Clare Strand

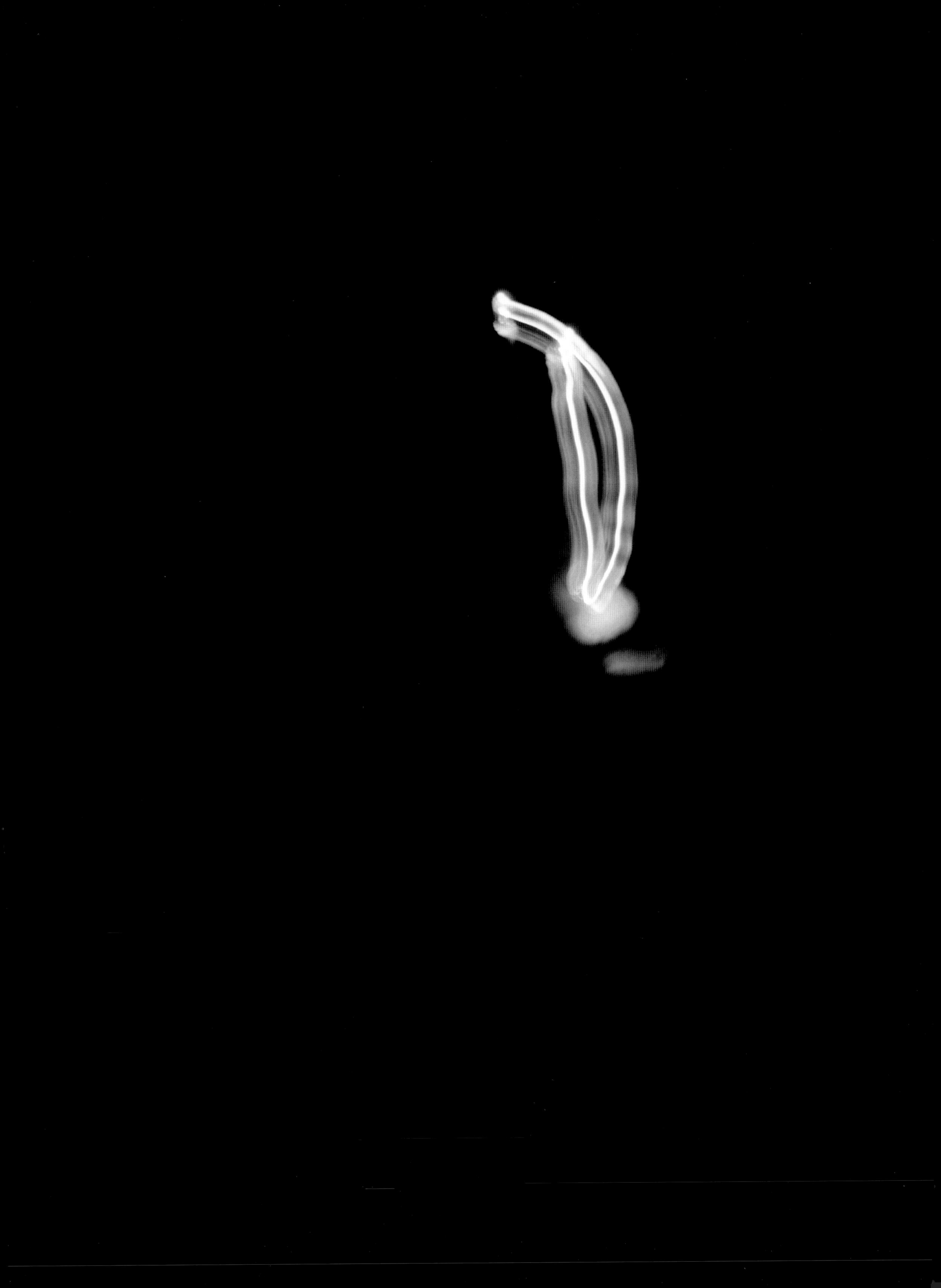

Clare Strand

A Photoworks Monograph

photoworks STEIDL

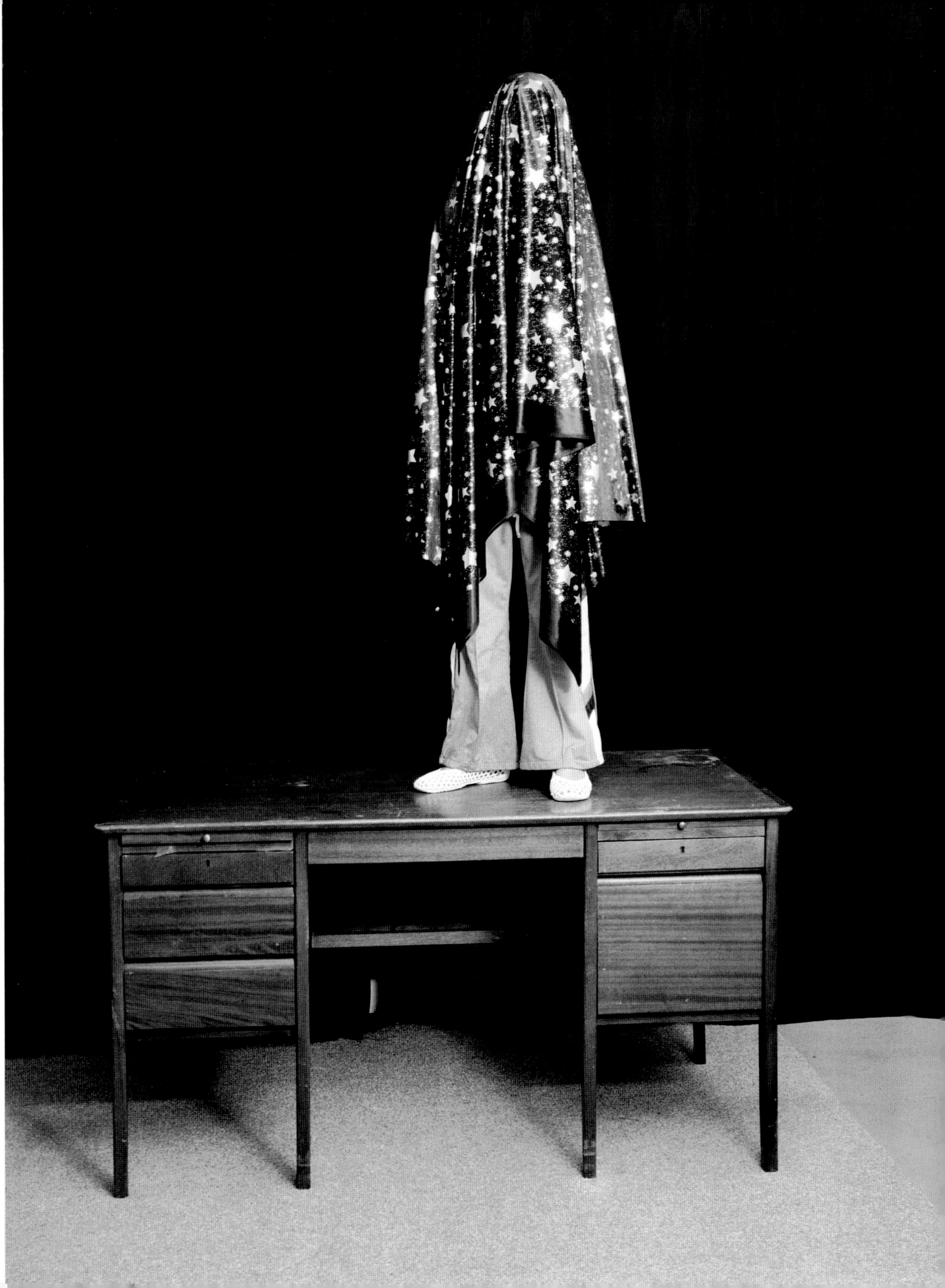

Foreword

Rebecca Drew

This is the sixth book in the Photoworks Monograph series co-published with Steidl. Each monograph surveys the work of an important emerging photographic artist in the UK, providing the first thorough account of their practice while acknowledging and celebrating their achievements to date. On this occasion, we present the extraordinary work of Clare Strand, to coincide with her major exhibition at the Museum Folkwang, Essen. Fascinated by phantasmagoria and trickery, Strand draws on vernacular photography to create a highly original visual language that is both humorous and philosophical. The cryptic series of works presented here continually keep us guessing, at once 'seductively curious' and 'funny peculiar'.

Collaboration is at the heart of all Photoworks productions and we are grateful to all those who have devoted their time and enthusiasm to this project. In particular, we would like to thank each of the writers for their perceptive engagement with Strand's work: Ute Eskildsen for teasing out Strand's fascination with photography's multiple meanings; Ian Jeffrey for his perceptive and erudite exploration of her philosophical tendencies and Chris Mullen for his insightful conversation with the artist, which delves into the mechanics of Strand's practice and unearths some of the inspirations for her work.

Our thanks, also, to all those who have enabled the reproduction of the numerous illustrative images in this book, which have contributed to making this such a rich and comprehensive investigation of the artist's practice. We are particularly grateful to John Hilliard and Thomas Ruff; Joel Sternfeld and Luhring Augustine, New York; National Gallery, Scotland; Getty Images and the International Centre of Photography; the Brassaï Estate; DACS and RMN; Peter Freedman Inc., New York; the Henry Moore Institute; Leeds Museums and Art Galleries and The Metropolitan Museum of Modern Art, New York.

This book would not have been possible without the continued involvement of key individuals and organisations. Firstly, we are grateful to Arts Council England for the ongoing support that has enabled this monograph series to be published. We would also like to acknowledge the expertise of our colleagues at Steidl, and extend our sincere thanks to Gerhard Steidl and Michael Mack. Our thanks as ever to Stuart Smith and his team at SMITH, who continue to design this series with unwavering attentiveness and style; to Benedict Burbridge and Gordon MacDonald for their invaluable input and to all our colleagues at Photoworks for their help and advice in the development of this book.

Most importantly, our thanks and appreciation to Clare Strand, who has contributed her vision, enthusiasm and incisive sense of humour to the production of this Photoworks Monograph.

Clare Strand: Vanity Fair

David Chandler

By the mid-1990s, if you were a young photographer in Britain looking for a direction and an identity for your work, the question of what to photograph – simply that – would have seemed a more pressing problem than ever. 'All the photographs have already been taken' was a commonly heard phrase of the time, a reference to a sense of exhaustion in the medium: not only, it seemed, had every angle, every style, every possible idea and approach already been used up, but also the act of photographing was increasingly regarded as unavoidably formulaic, seeing was effectively compromised by overbearing visual traditions and inventions, old and new. Our culture had been saturated with photographs for generations; as the artist Joachim Schmid would say, 'there were too many photographs already, why take more?' Added to this so much contemporary photography in Britain was still in the grip of a form of didacticism that had evolved from the deconstructive practices of conceptual art, much of it linked to the new body of critical theory developed through the 1970s. Photography in this post-conceptual climate – deemed valueless in itself, a redundant formal language – must now reconstruct its worthiness and relevance by its application either to overt social and political concerns or to the inherent phenomenological problems of the medium. As young aspiring photographers considered what untapped issues they might confront, or pondered how they might best refute some photographic truism, photography as an art form seemed full of road blocks and aspirations became more bound up with scales of production, success afforded to those who were the most effective managers, mobilising resources – locations, studios, props, actors, and funds – like film directors, something which both reflected the increasing influence of film on contemporary photographers and for many defined where their ambitions were heading.

Within this sense of stasis, however, were signs of a change of spirit. Just as the variety of oppositional voices that had found a common enemy in Margaret Thatcher had begun to dissipate, especially after her resignation in 1990, so the photographic consensus began to shift away from overtly issue-based practices, towards more diverse personal and political concerns, within which there was more room for the experiential, the diaristic, the playfully irreverent and aesthetically bold. The emergence of Wolfgang Tillmans, for example, who had his first show at the influential Maureen Paley Gallery in London, in 1993, was indicative of this change. Working across fashion, art and documentary, Tillmans' ecstatic installations were unapologetically intuitive and uninhibited in their celebration of photography's expanded vocabulary. It was a kind of rehabilitation of the photograph's visual potential and immediacy.

Allied to this, it was the more anarchic, mischievous legacy of conceptualism, rather than its critical austerity, that seemed newly relevant: the work of Americans Bruce Nauman, John Baldessari, Robert Smithson and Ed Ruscha, for example, or the more recent example of artists as diverse as Jeff Wall, Gabriel Orozco and Roman Signer. Also, in British conceptual art of the late 1960s and early 70s, the undermining of photography's claim to objective truth did not necessarily preclude a sense of playful anarchy and absurdism. The pioneering work of Keith Arnatt and John Hilliard, for example, which blended various performative strategies with photographic experimentation, analysis and documentation, now offered a distinct point of reference for a younger generation then finding their way through the photographic maze.

It is in this context that we might usefully consider the work of Clare Strand, who graduated from the first year of Brighton University's new photography BA degree course in 1995. As a teenager in the 1980s, Strand was not particularly interested in contemporary art – photographic, conceptual or otherwise – but was drawn instead to the disturbed surfaces of ordinary life as dramatised in popular culture: in crime stories – real and fictional, in the paranormal, in Hollywood horror films such as *The Exorcist* (1973), *Carrie* (1976) and *The Watcher in the Wood* (1980), and in the weird news and strange phenomena of *Fortean Times*. This interest in the macabre, both for itself and as a social preoccupation and source of fantasy, has remained central to her work, and has helped establish the tone of her own particular form of photographic irreverence. Strand's photography

John Hilliard, *Describing a Trajectory 1: Camera as Projectile*, 1971.

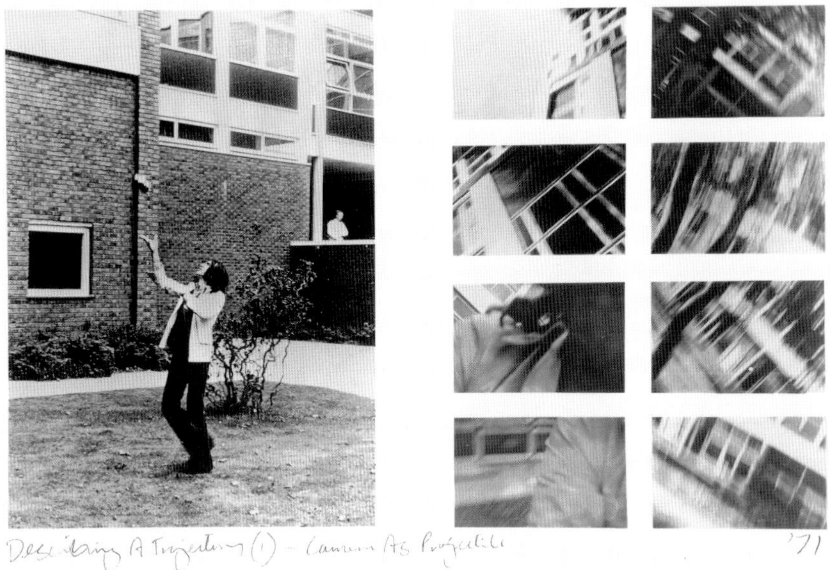

does not adhere easily to any particular genre. Indeed it is her dislike of photography's ordering tendency, its often too rigid categorisations and its still complacent values and traditions, that has underpinned the development of her work. But Strand's art is not severe or hectoring in its criticisms, her approach is never doctrinaire; rather it adopts that playfully subversive quality mentioned above, that freedom to experiment and to reinvent at will the ground rules of what might be seen as serious photographic practice. It is exemplary in this respect of a new liberated and imaginative sensibility in British photography (of which Tillmans might now be seen as a senior figure), that could be defined as a willingness to embrace photography in all its forms, to travel through and rearrange its history, to be sly or straightforward or both together, or to be absurd for the sake of it. While this work rails against photographic orthodoxy, and authority, it is also a form of celebration of photography's beguiling ability to communicate very directly, to make us think even if not to clarify our understanding. The work might even embody a form of social or political commentary, a satire perhaps, but in reserving the right to be critical or simply unsettling, it always resists being pinned to some theoretical or analytical display board.

Since 2001, Strand has completed a series of highly distinctive projects, which range over that broad panoply of photography's past and present. Each body of work, from *Gone Astray* to the most recent *Unseen Agents*, takes its inspiration and initial co-ordinates from a particular photographic genre, from Victorian studio portraiture, or forensic photography, to the camera's adventures with the paranormal. The works gain a certain poise and weight from their historical associations but also an indeterminacy: they are difficult to place and to date, situating themselves at odd angles to photography's grand narrative while gently pulling at the threads that might unravel it.

In the *Gone Astray Portraits*, for example, there is an air of pastiche, as Strand places character types from contemporary London's streets against a painted backdrop of a woodland glade that evokes the studio settings of nineteenth-century portraitists. Each figure bears the traces of disarray or physical harm, but they are also unperturbed

Gone Astray Portraits

2002–2003

I had romantic ideas in connection with that religious edifice; firmly believing that all the beggars who pretended through the week to be blind, lame, deaf and dumb, and otherwise physically afflicted, laid aside their pretences every Sunday, dressed themselves in holiday clothes and attended divine service in the temple of their patron saint.

Charles Dickens, 'Gone Astray', *Household Words*, 13th August 1853.

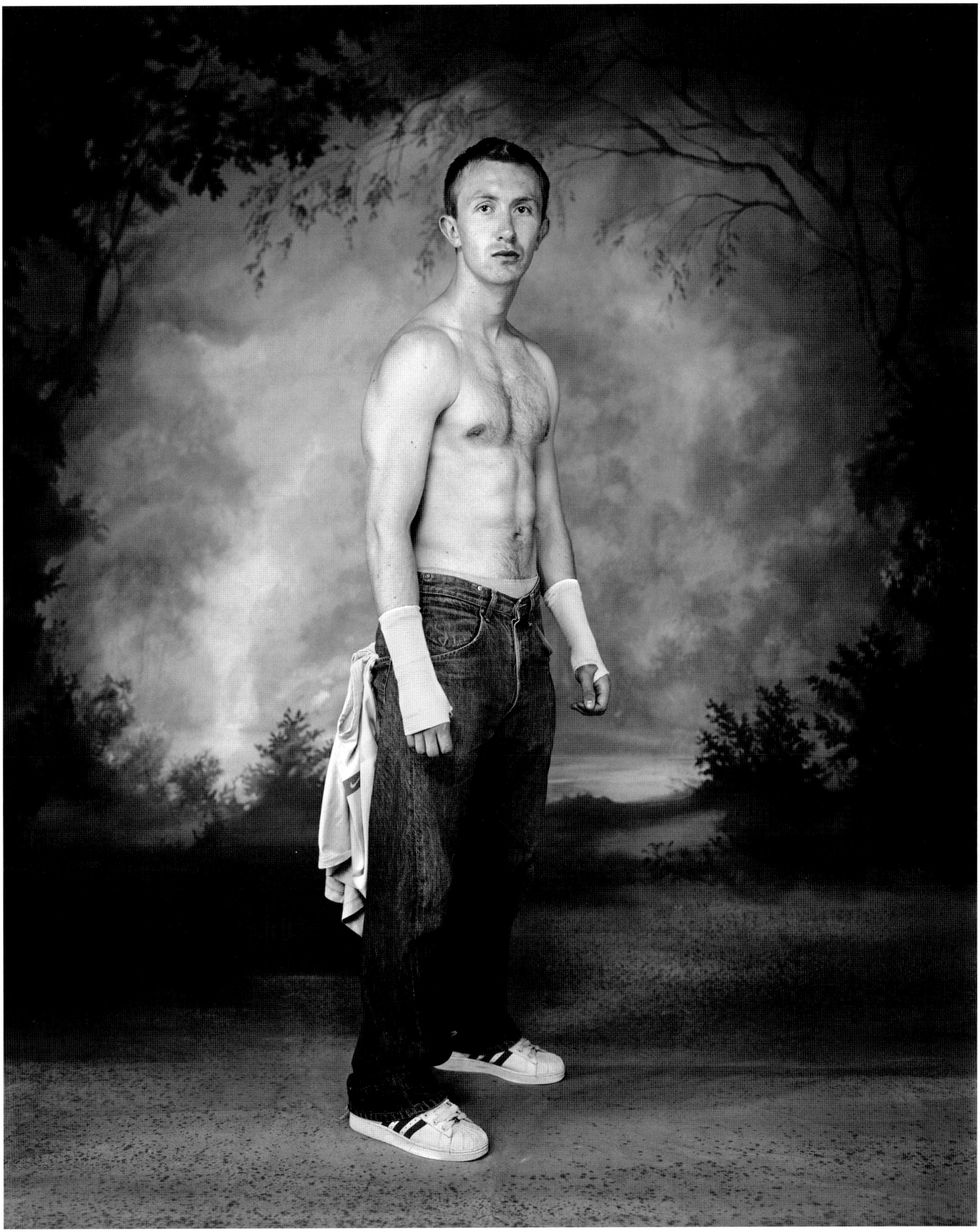

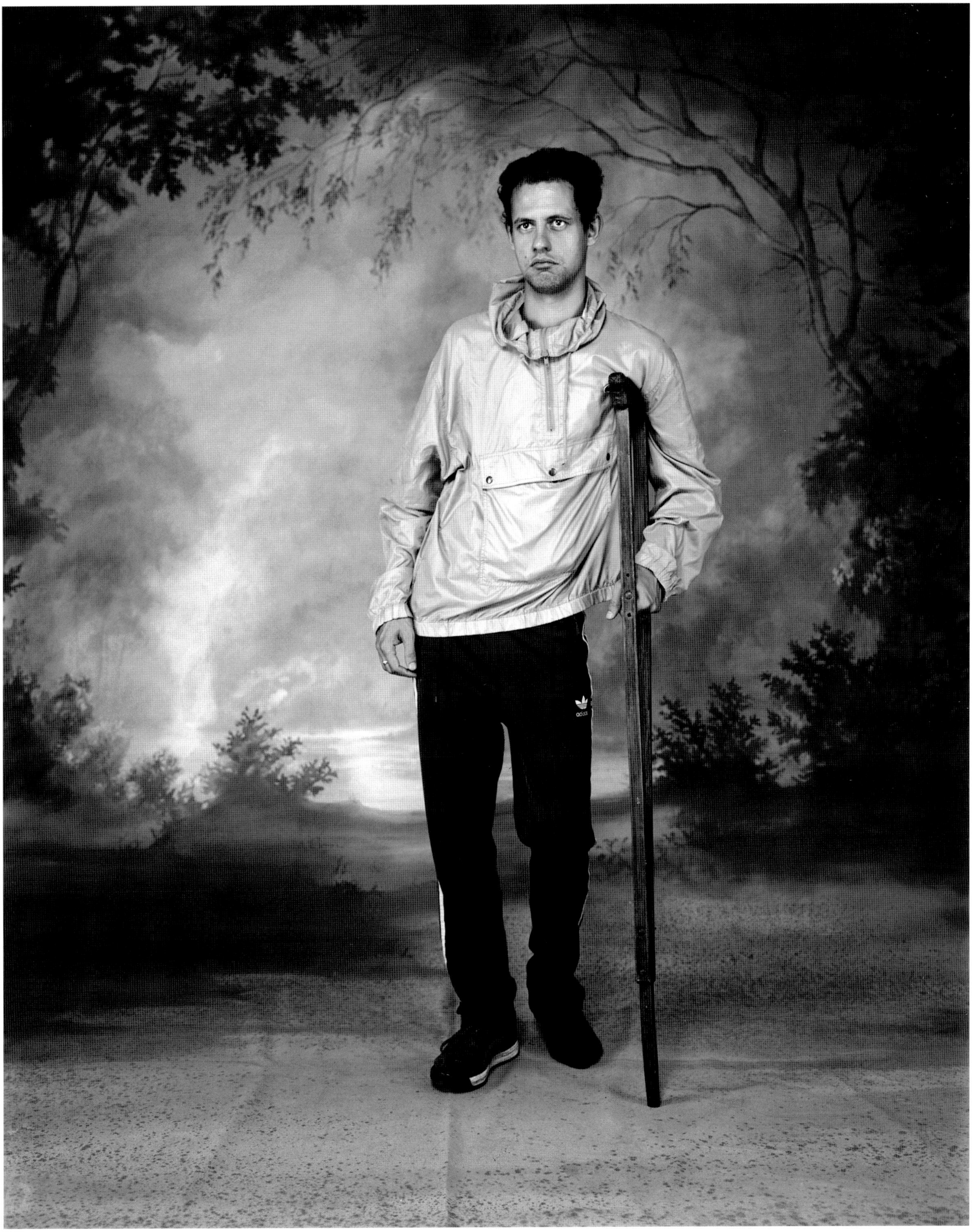

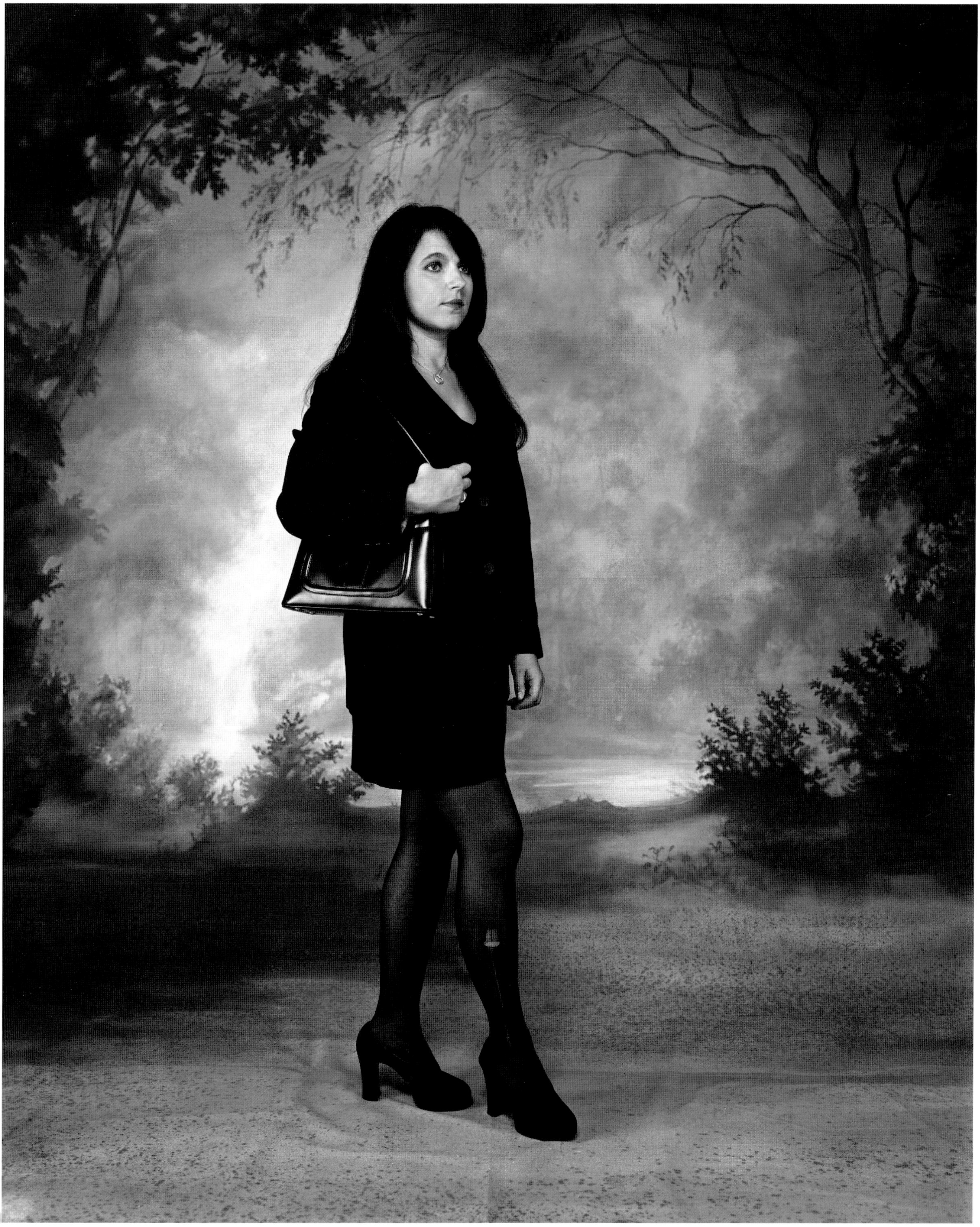

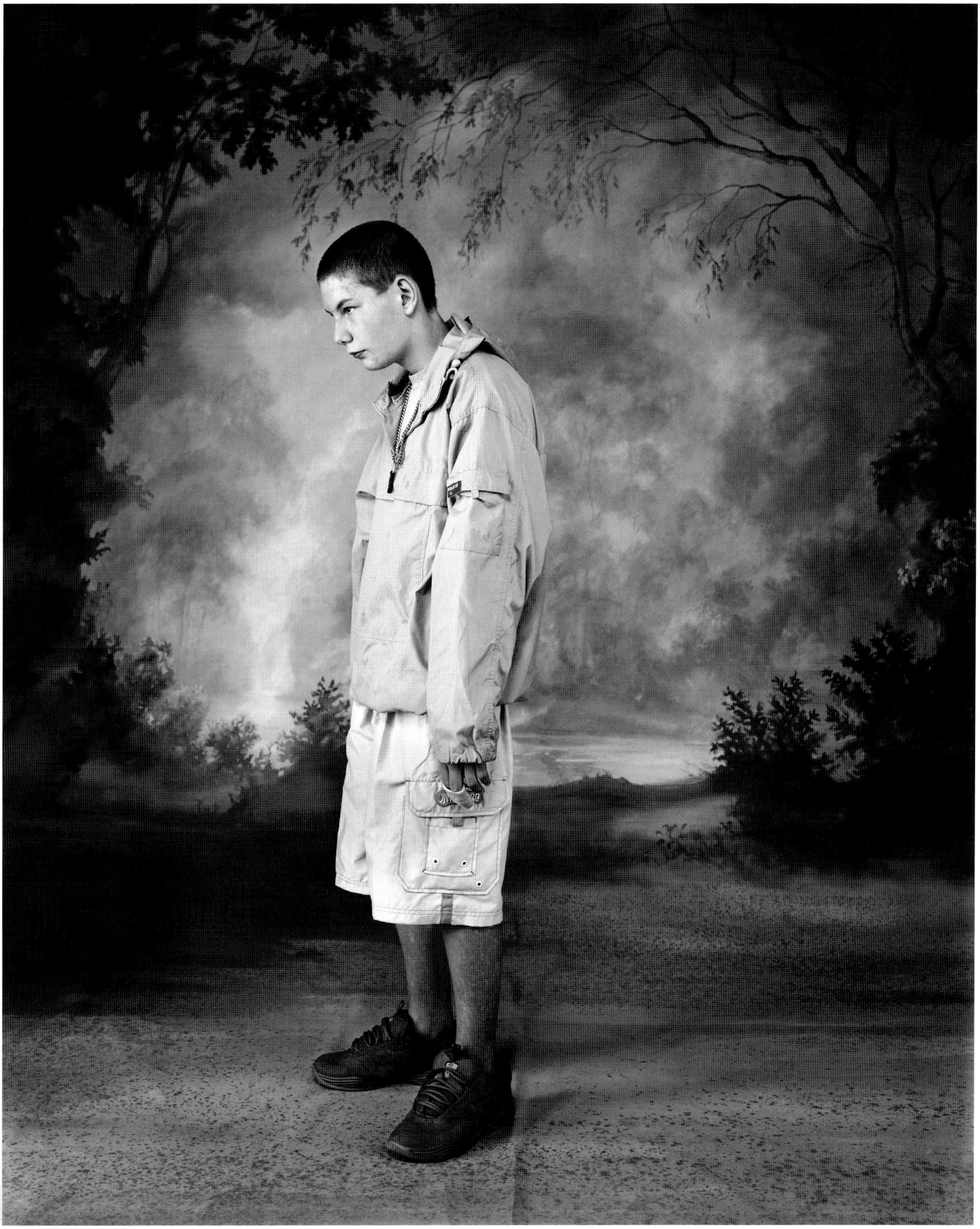

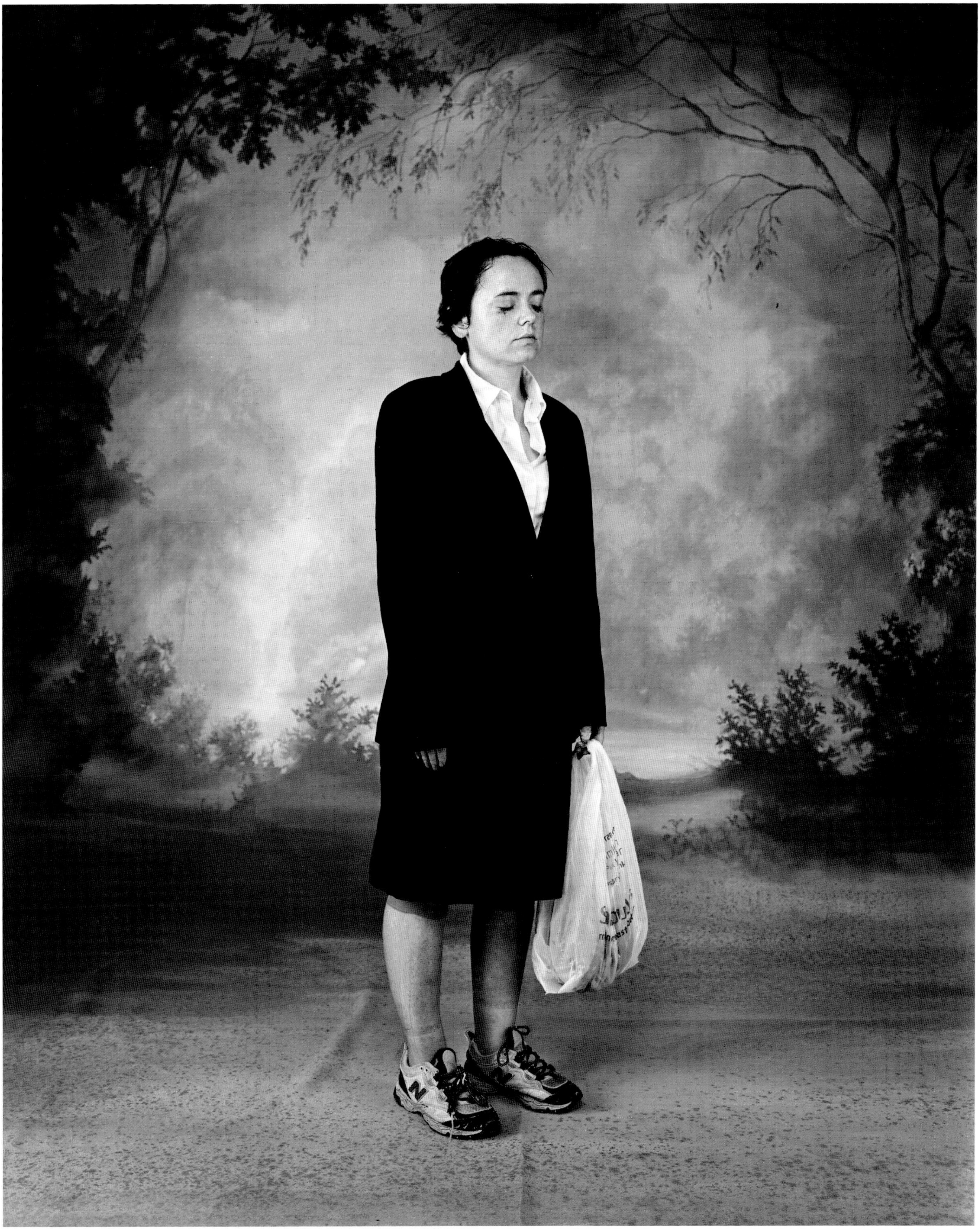

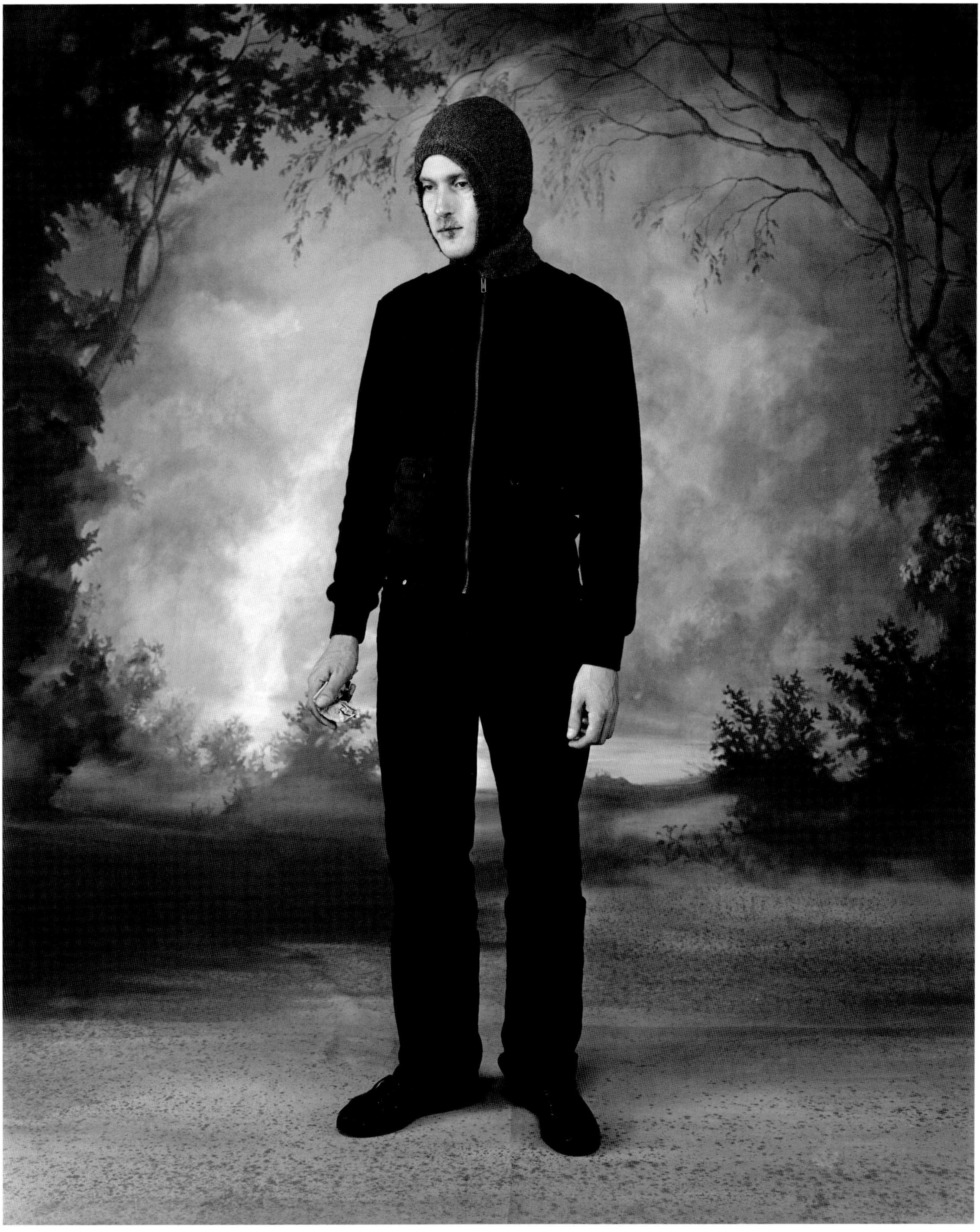

Gone Astray Details

2002 – 2003

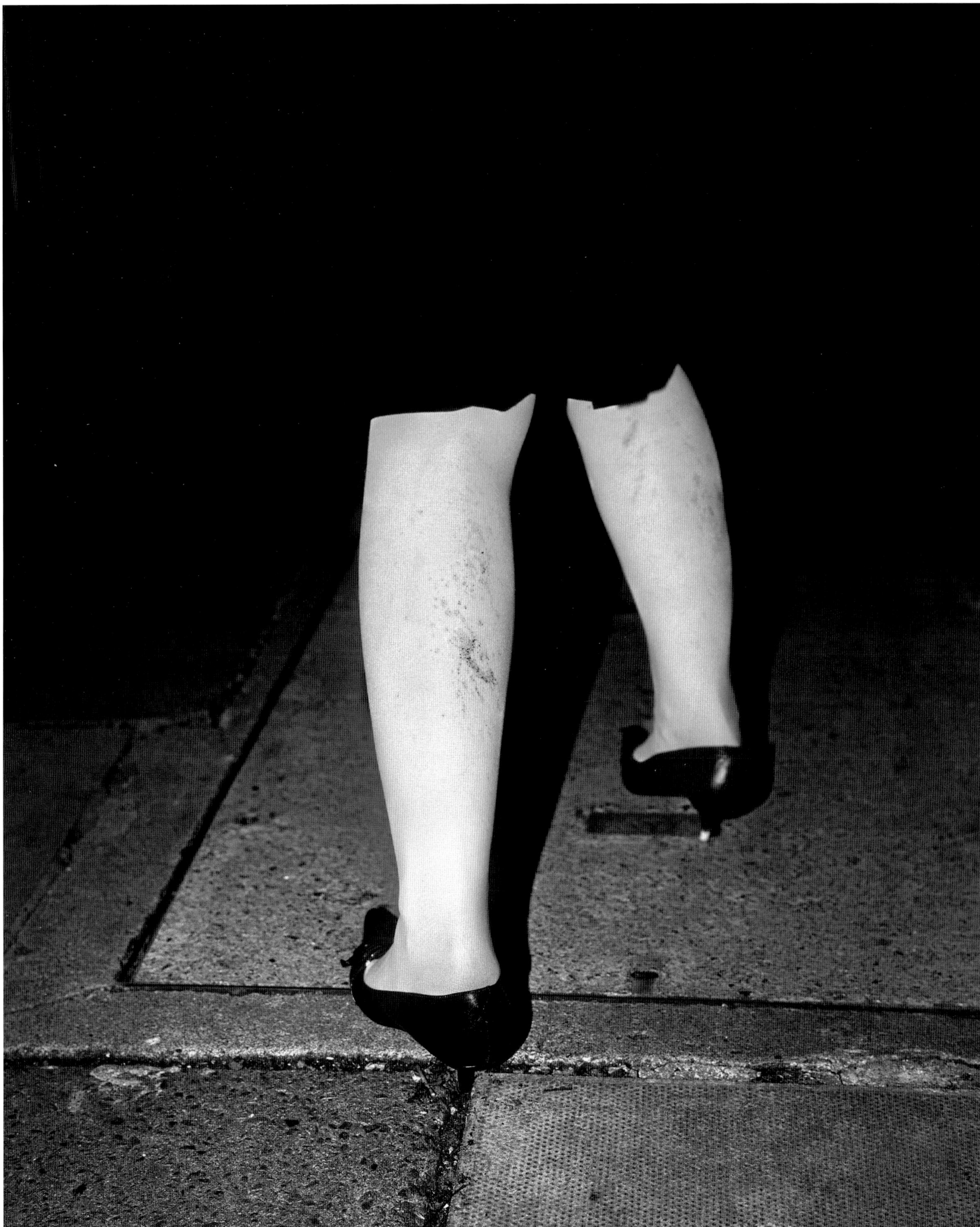

Short Stories 1–9 **1** On the corner of Bowling Green Lane a mididle aged woman suddenly fell to her knees on the pavement. There was no

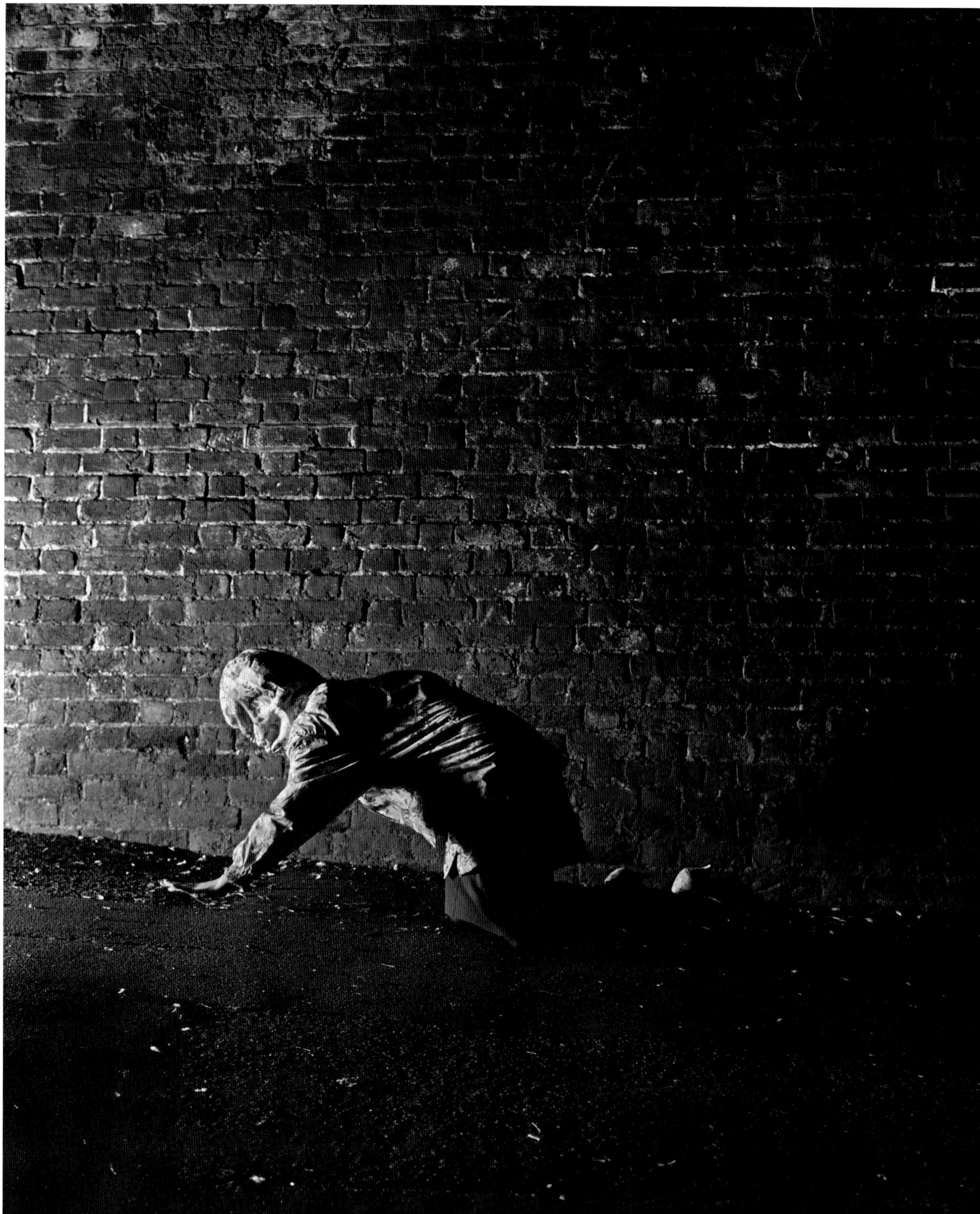

laughed, another understood without question and the third looked out of the window and thought about dead foxes. **3** At 7am on Cowcross

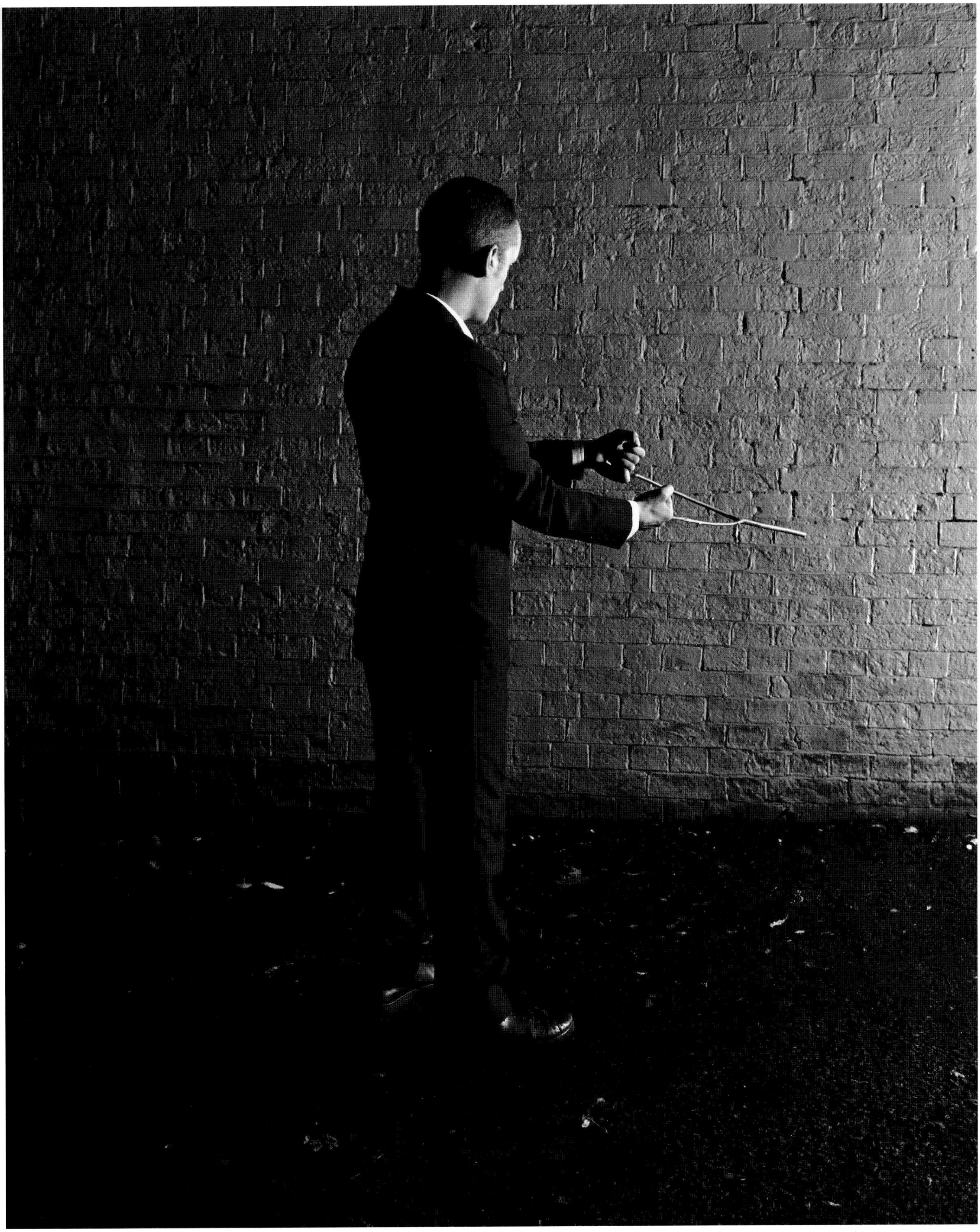

Street three manhole covers were found to have been tampered with by persons unknown during the night. **4** At 9.33pm the woman was seen crossing the Green. A young boy recalled seeing her come to a sudden halt then bend down making a tugging action with her arms. He said

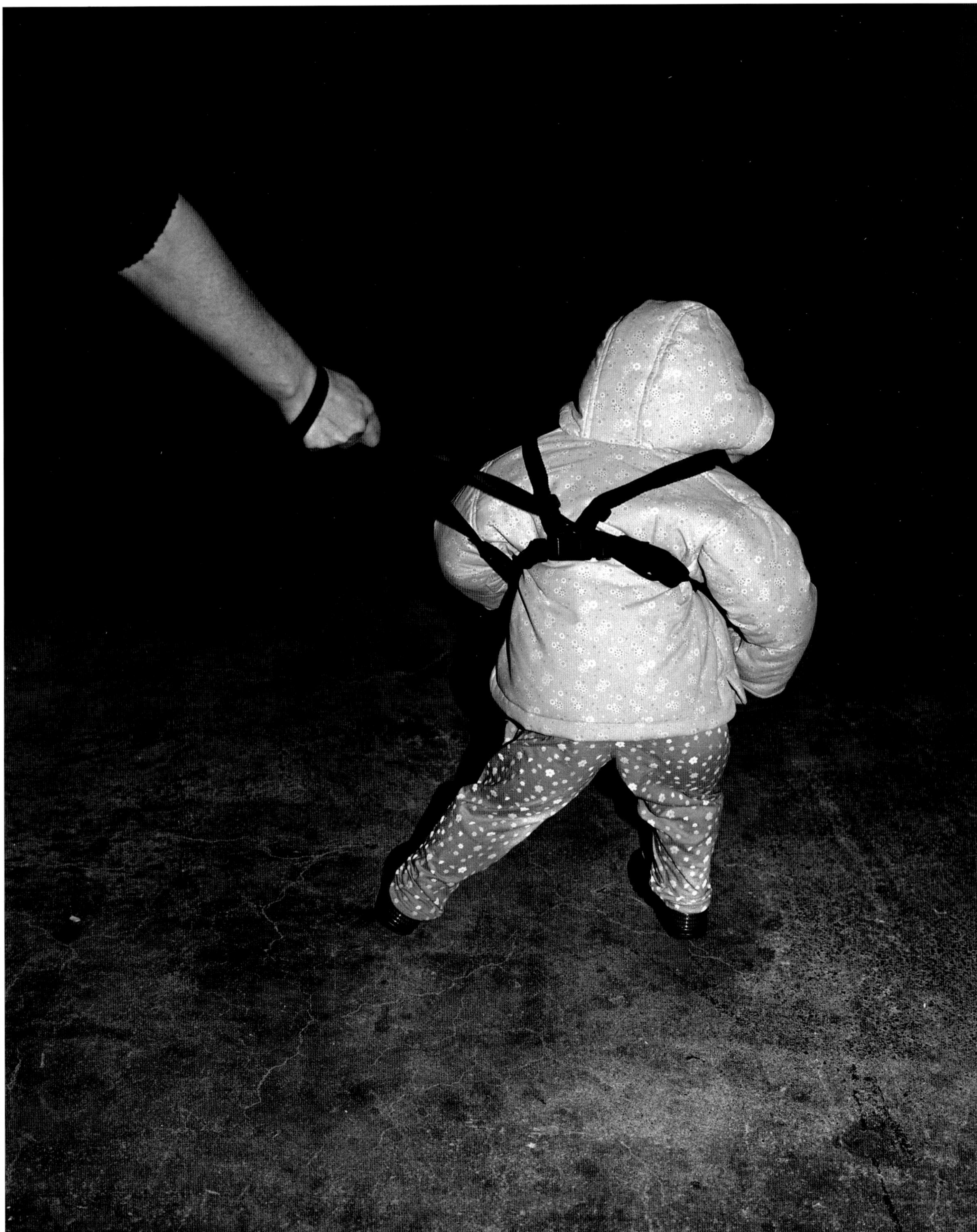

sh she looked confused and he was surprised she wasn't wearing a coat. **5** Members attended the investigation. The group included some with

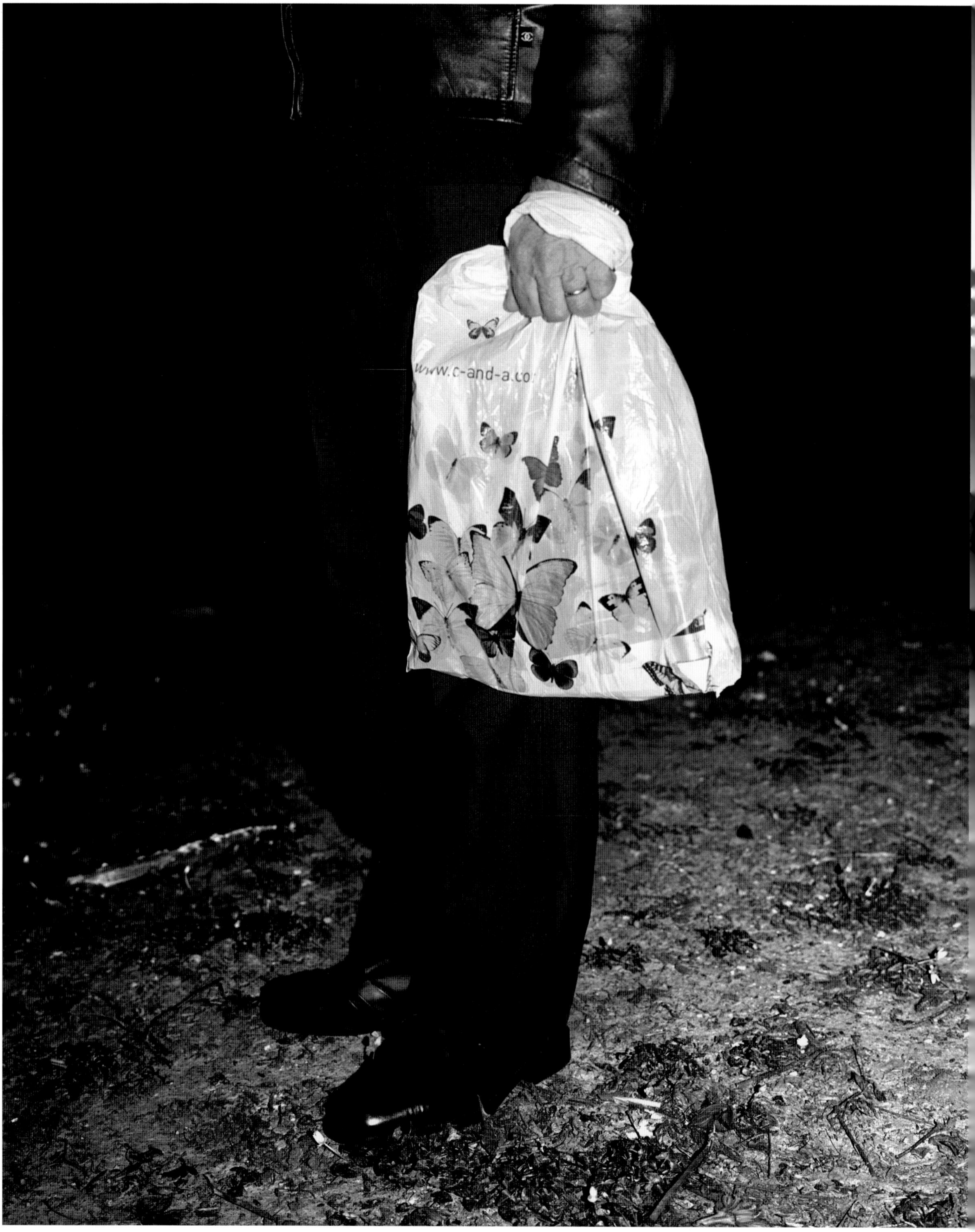

crucial instruction. This however did not deter her and the illusion was performed to her satisfaction. Later she confessed she could not be

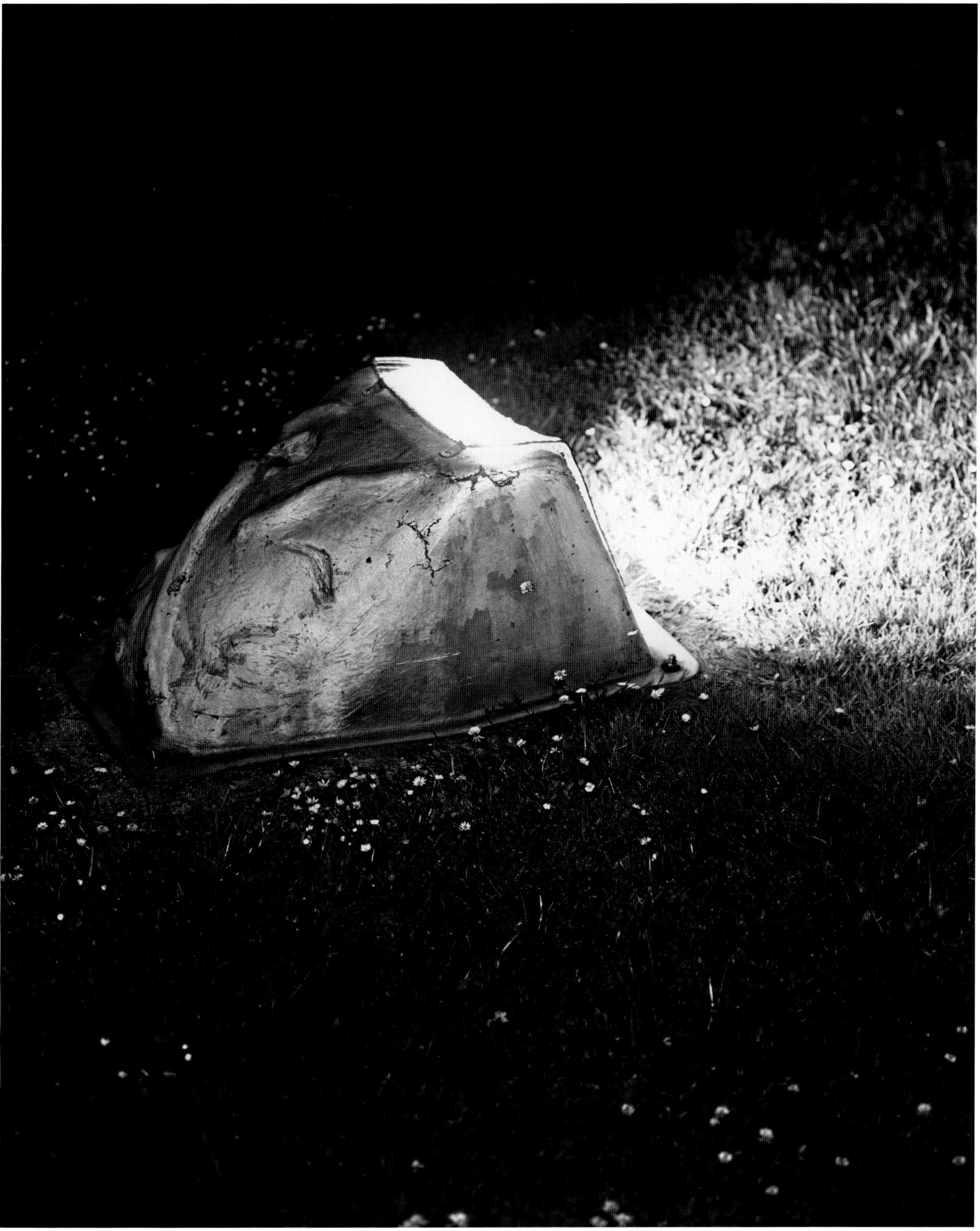

sure. **7** A married man rubbed the top of his head in a circular action then wiped his right eye dragging the lower lid along and off to the right.

He was heard saying how he wished things would stop changing and instead stay the same... He was later seen on the corner of Saffron Hill

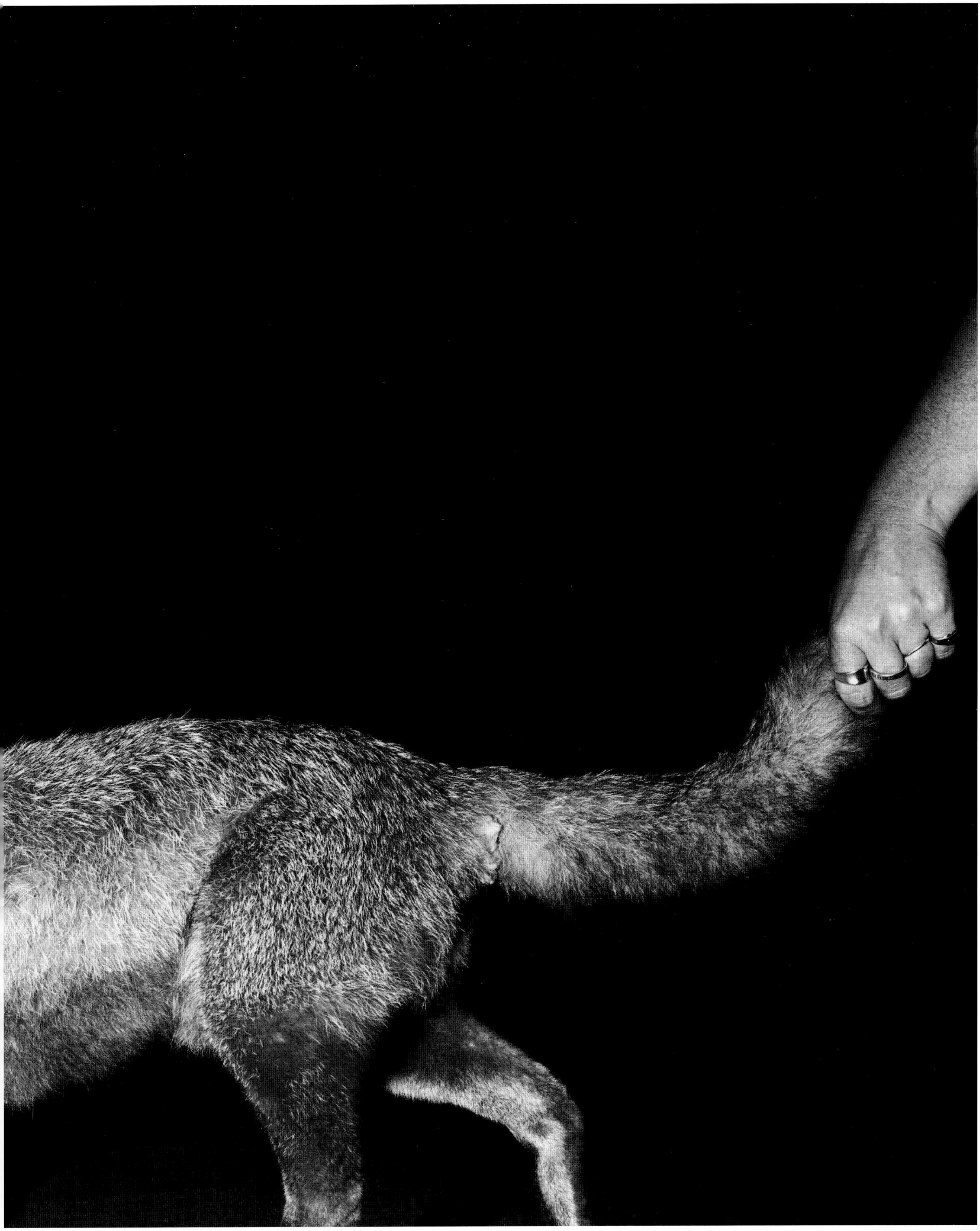

heading North. **8** It prefers rich soils and therefore does well around settlements benefiting from the waste we produce – often indicating where old settlements have long since disappeared from the countryside. **9** A pair of child's sodden Wellington boots are found in the Pear

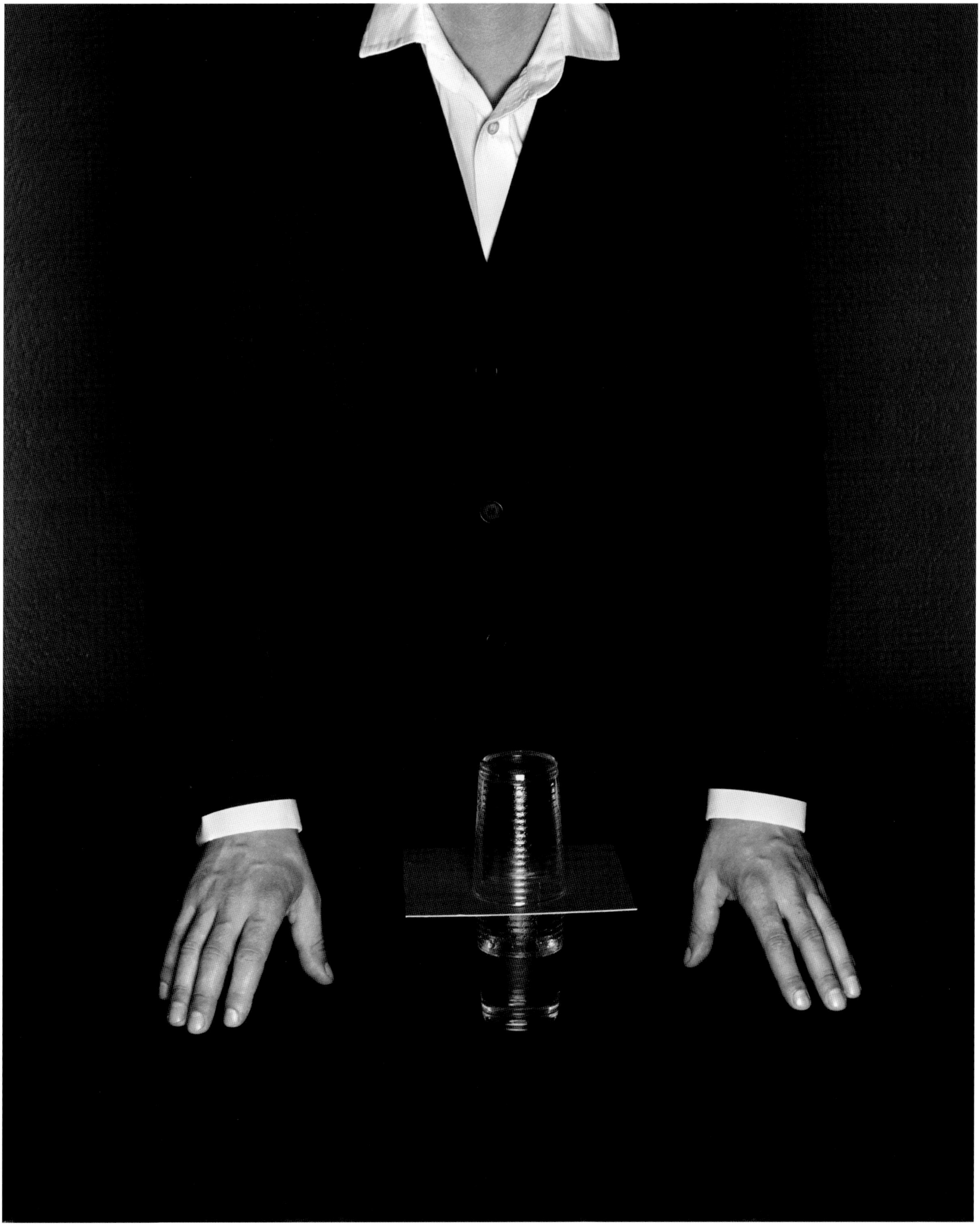

Tree Court area every other Monday morning. Residents have reported hearing a young child's cries, but no sightings have been made.

News from Photography

Ute Eskildsen

'He who reveals any hint of his secret no longer has the Other in his power.' Jean Paul (1763–1825)

Clare Strand works with photographs she has taken herself and also others that she finds, collects and incorporates into themed series. Since childhood she has been fascinated by crime stories, horror and the paranormal. In interviews she often refers to the films and literature that influenced her in youth, convinced that 'what gets you in adolescent life remains with you forever'.[1]

On the face of it, Strand might seem to be creating difficulties for herself by working with the medium historically credited with producing the most accurate representation of its subjects. Given that photography has subsequently come to be regarded as providing only limited authenticity, why concentrate on such a medium? Is she just tilting at windmills, or rather, does she organise her ideas by means of a tried and tested conceptual framework that she brings to bear on her themed series, giving expression to her vision with these representations?

Clare Strand is not driven to take photographs for their own sake. She begins by researching a

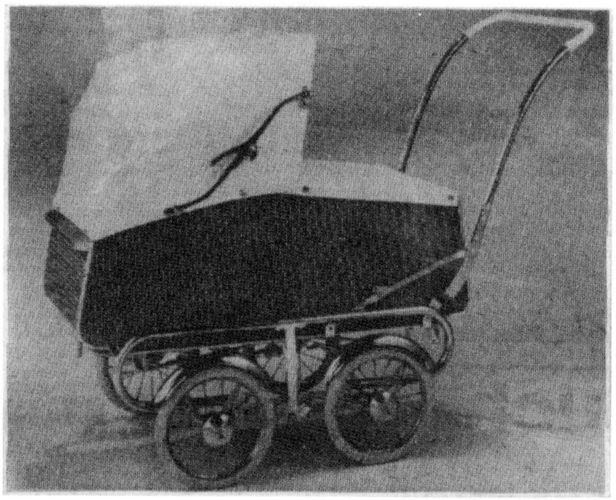

Thomas Ruff, *Zeitungsfoto 021*, 1992.

particular subject, which arises from her own experiences of life, from her reading and observations, and from her extensive knowledge of the history of photography. The latter is significant as she is not one of those photographic artists who develop and hone a successful style of image-making, instead she works out a method which is most suited to each specific theme. As Strand says, 'I have always found it helpful to understand how I can use photography through an appreciation of utilitarian images.'[2]

Strand's interest in utilitarian photography is also found in the work of the German photographer Thomas Ruff, who since the early 1980s has been finding points of reference for his work in the history of photography. Despite the great thematic and formalistic differences in their pictures (colour versus black and white for instance), the works of both artists raise similar questions, reflecting on the conditions of the process of taking photographs, the inherent meaning of representations, and the relationship between artistic activity and the practice of photography. Both produce thematic bodies of work which question the significance of the positioning of individual pictures within a series. Strand in particular is interested in the limited extent to which a photographic image can be read: 'I am drawn to images that contain visual codes appearing to explain but which actually don't really help at all.'[3] She is galvanized by the inability of the photographic process to ever actually achieve the accuracy of likeness that it had long seemed to promise and even to deliver.

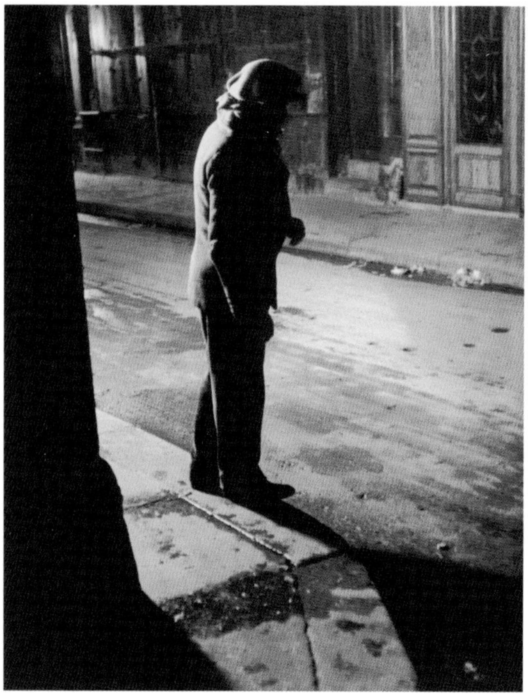

Brassaï, *The escaped con one evening on the Rue de la Ferronnerie in Les Halles*, 1932.

Weegee, *A drunk lying on the pavement outside the Dunhill Funeral Home in New York City, 31 December 1943.*

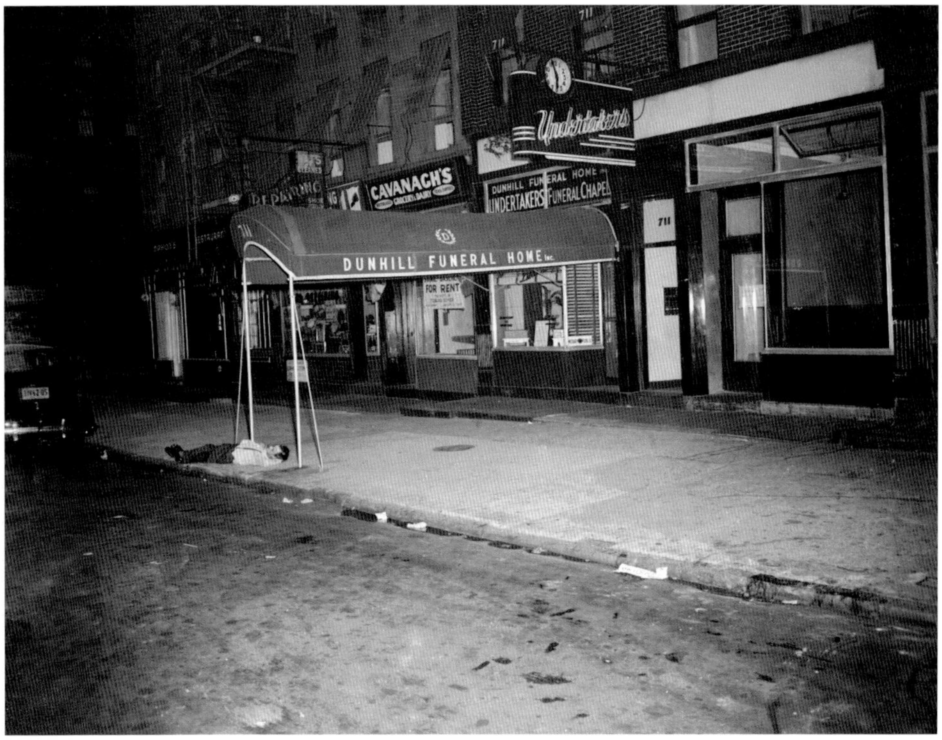

What is the significance of the sequence and the context for the supposed readability of Clare Strand's work, for example in the collections *Gone Astray Details* (2002–2003) and *Signs of a Struggle* (2003)? *Gone Astray*, a title taken from Charles Dickens' *Household Words*, is a two-part series, commissioned by the London College of Communication about the area of Clerkenwell in London, which, for Strand, is a microcosm of the metropolis: a magical, complex arena and the setting for historical events and stories. *Gone Astray Portraits*, which was produced in the studio, depicts various contemporary urban characters, full-length, dressed in their everyday clothes, posed in front of backdrops painted with landscapes reminiscent of the nineteenth century. Are these people representatives of particular 'types', the man or woman in the street, or actors? Playing with isolated figures in this way, taking them out of their urban context and social roles and placing them in front of a theatrical stage set, demonstrates Strand's fascination with uncertainty and the multiple meanings of photographs.

The second part of this work, *Gone Astray Details*, consists of ten photographs taken at night, each one showing a different mysterious scene, enacted either by Clare Strand herself or her partner. For example, we see a large tub containing a plant that is being touched by a small, graceful hand, or the rear view of a woman's legs with indeterminate markings on the skin, or a man holding a divining rod in front of a painted wall. In other photographs we see a child in a harness, again from the rear, and a figure on all fours – is it a woman? Is her face disfigured or is she wearing a mask? Has she fallen, or has she just crawled out of her hiding place? The lighting, usually flashlight, is a very important aspect of this process, heightening the artificiality of the situation.

These are mysterious pictures whose strangeness is at the same time reminiscent of other photographs or even books: *Paris at Night* (1932) by Brassaï, for example, or *Dunhill Funeral Home*, a picture from Weegee's *Naked City* (1945). The night as an urban stage peopled with a quite different cast of characters or the unknown city by night as a crime scene – in these contexts too Clare is working with

The Betterment Room –
Devices For Measuring Achievement

2004–2005

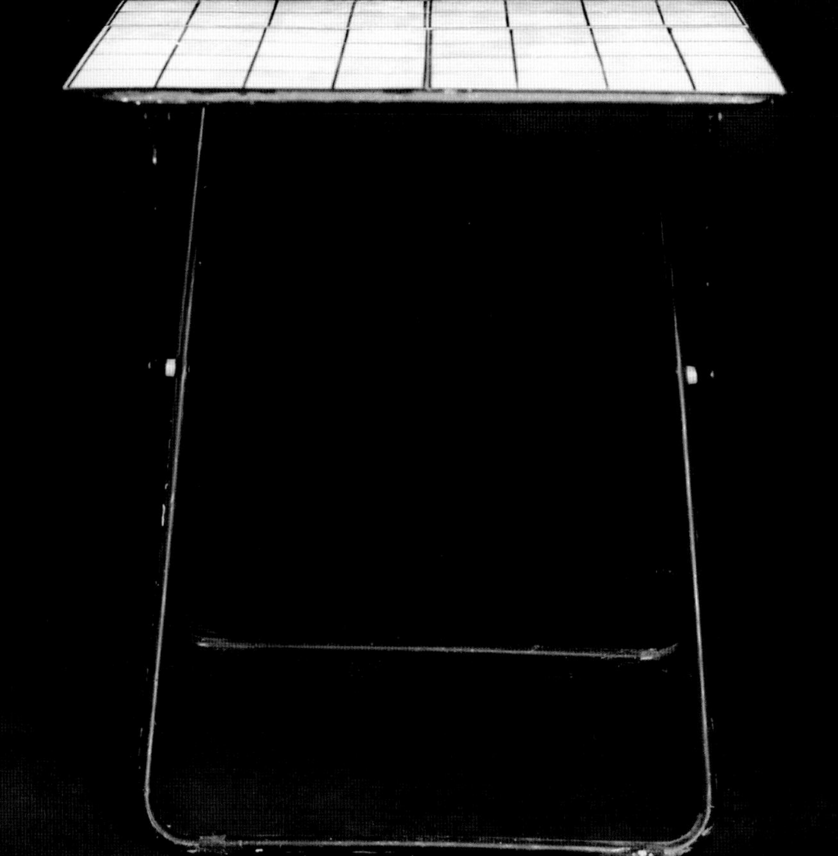

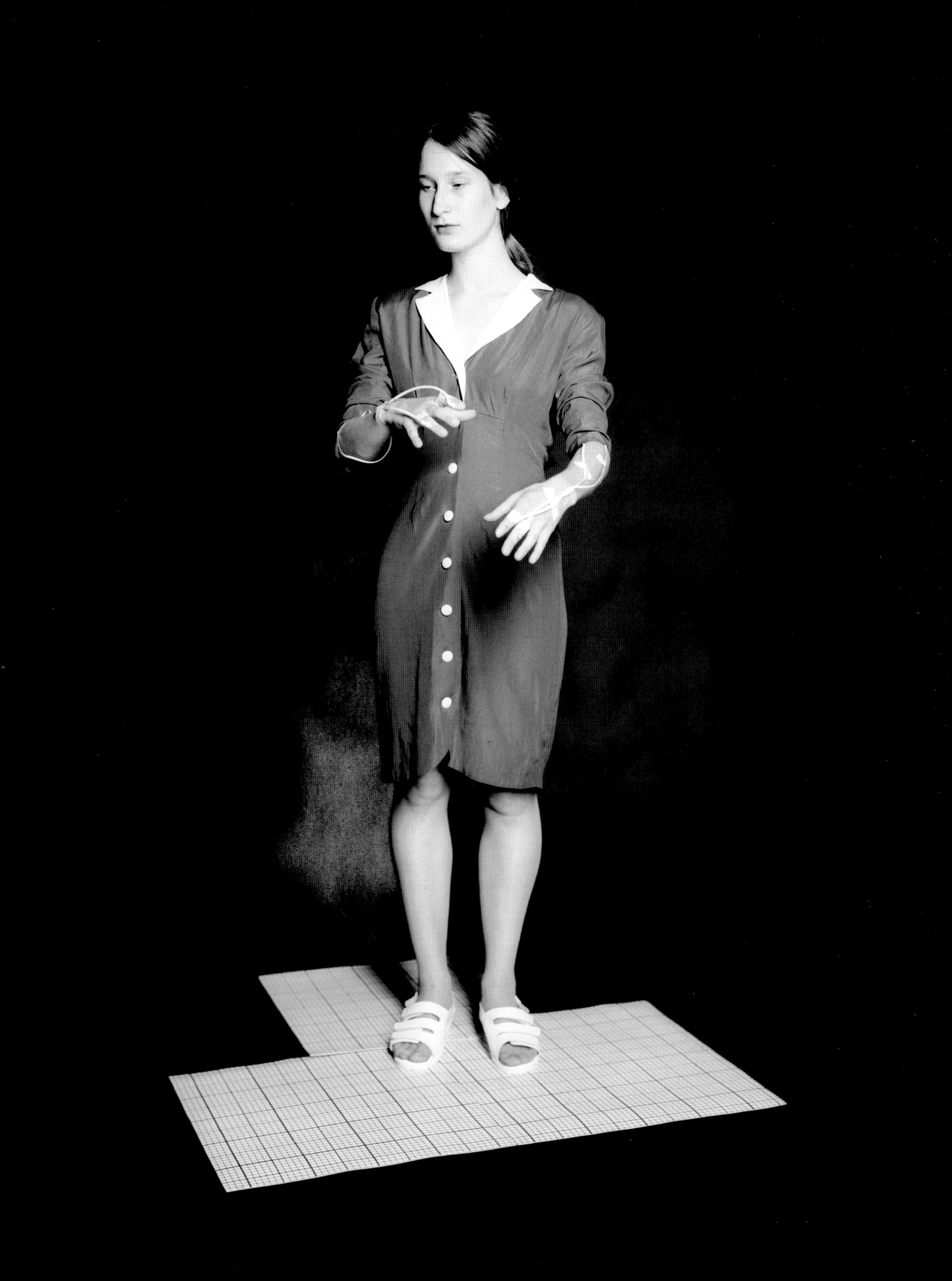

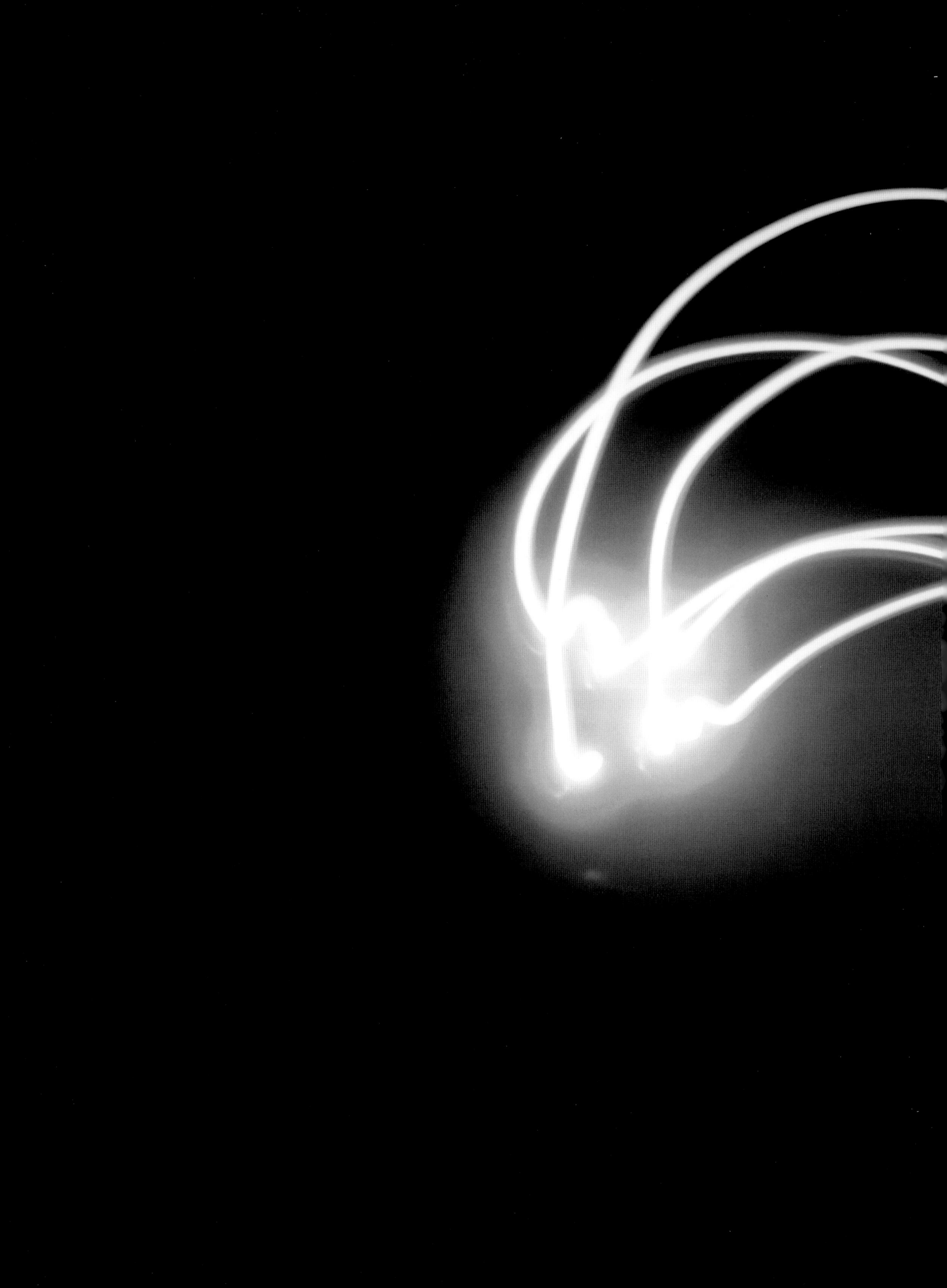

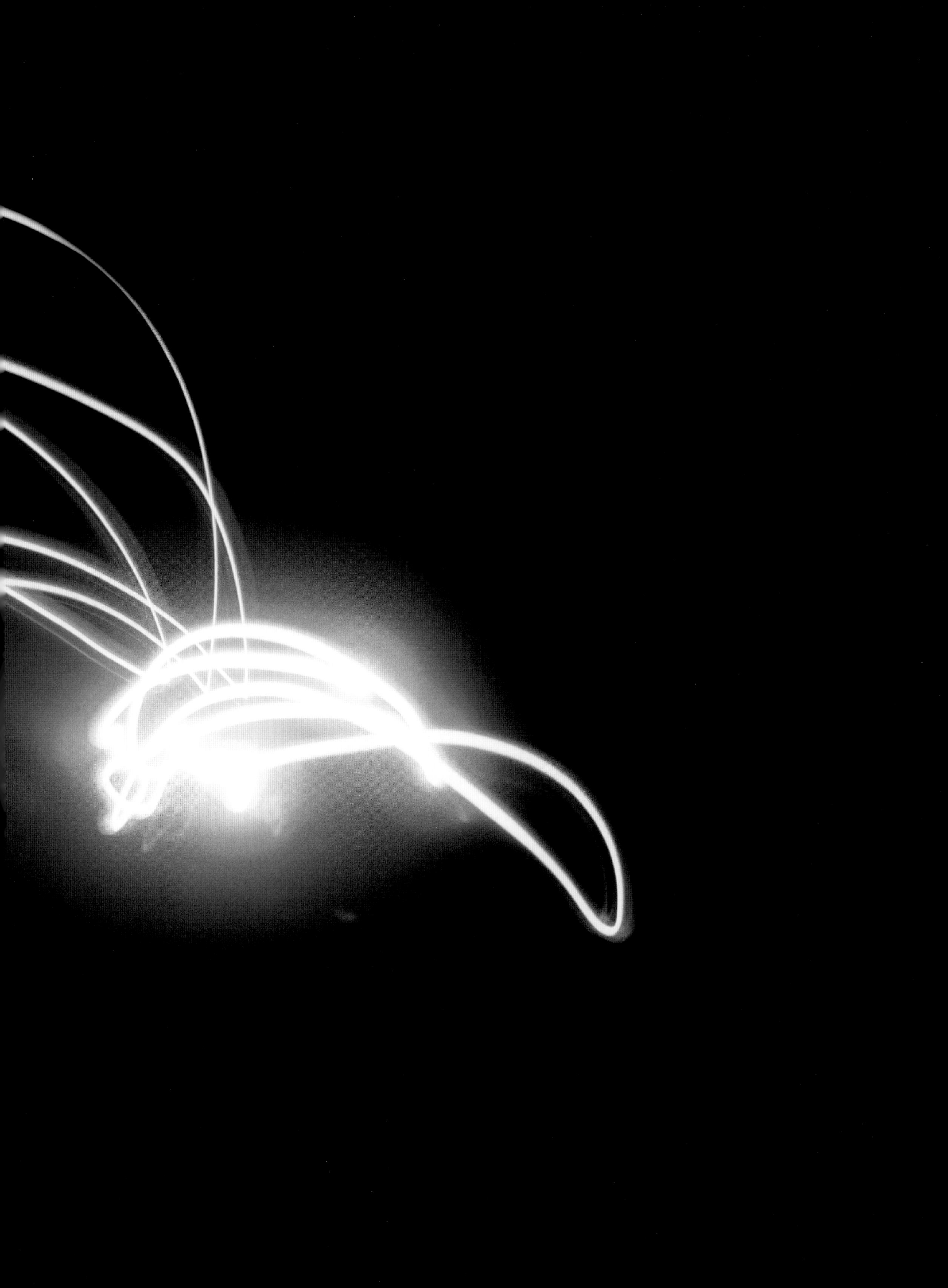

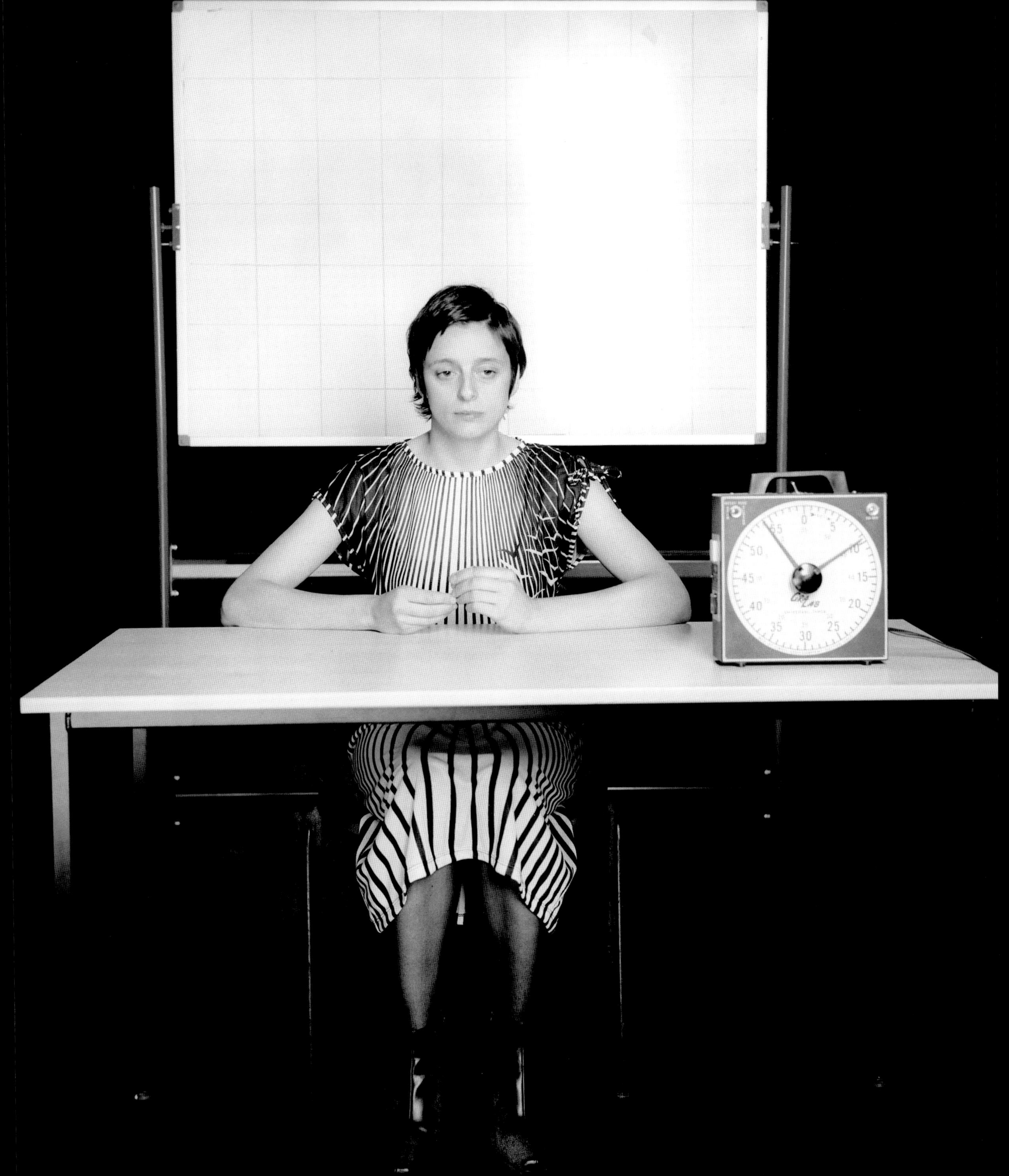
0 5 10 15 20 25 30 35 40 45 50 55

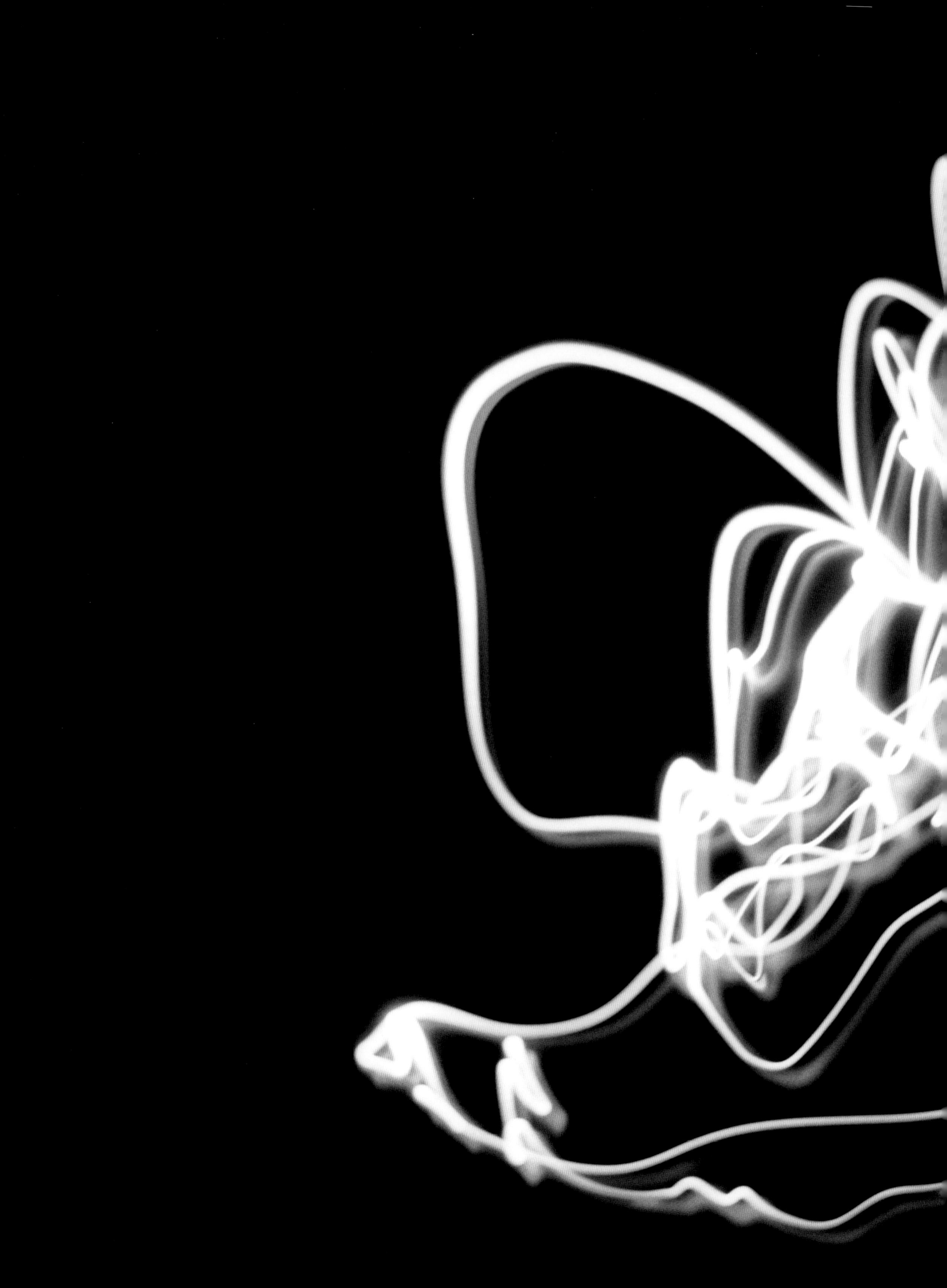

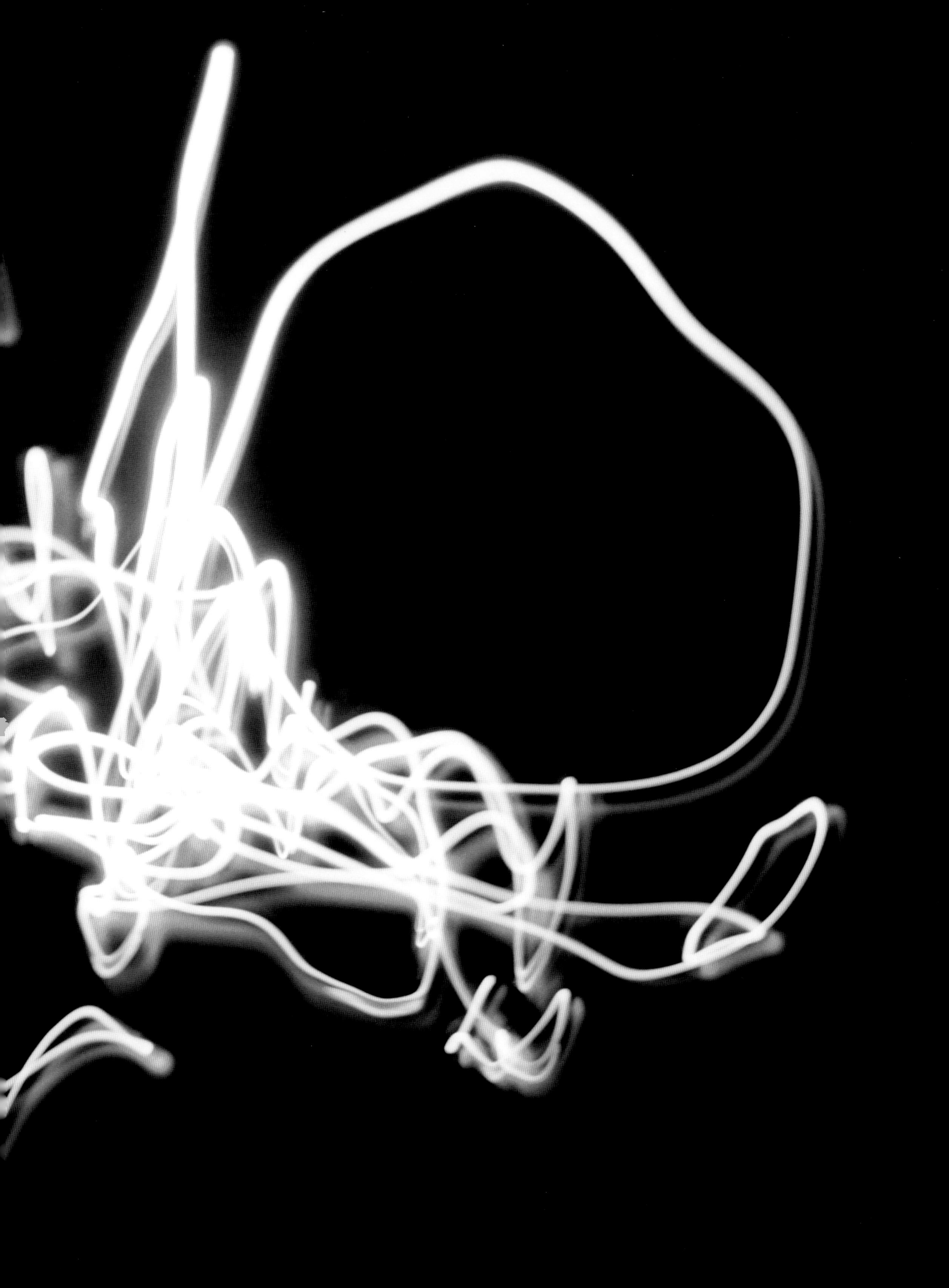

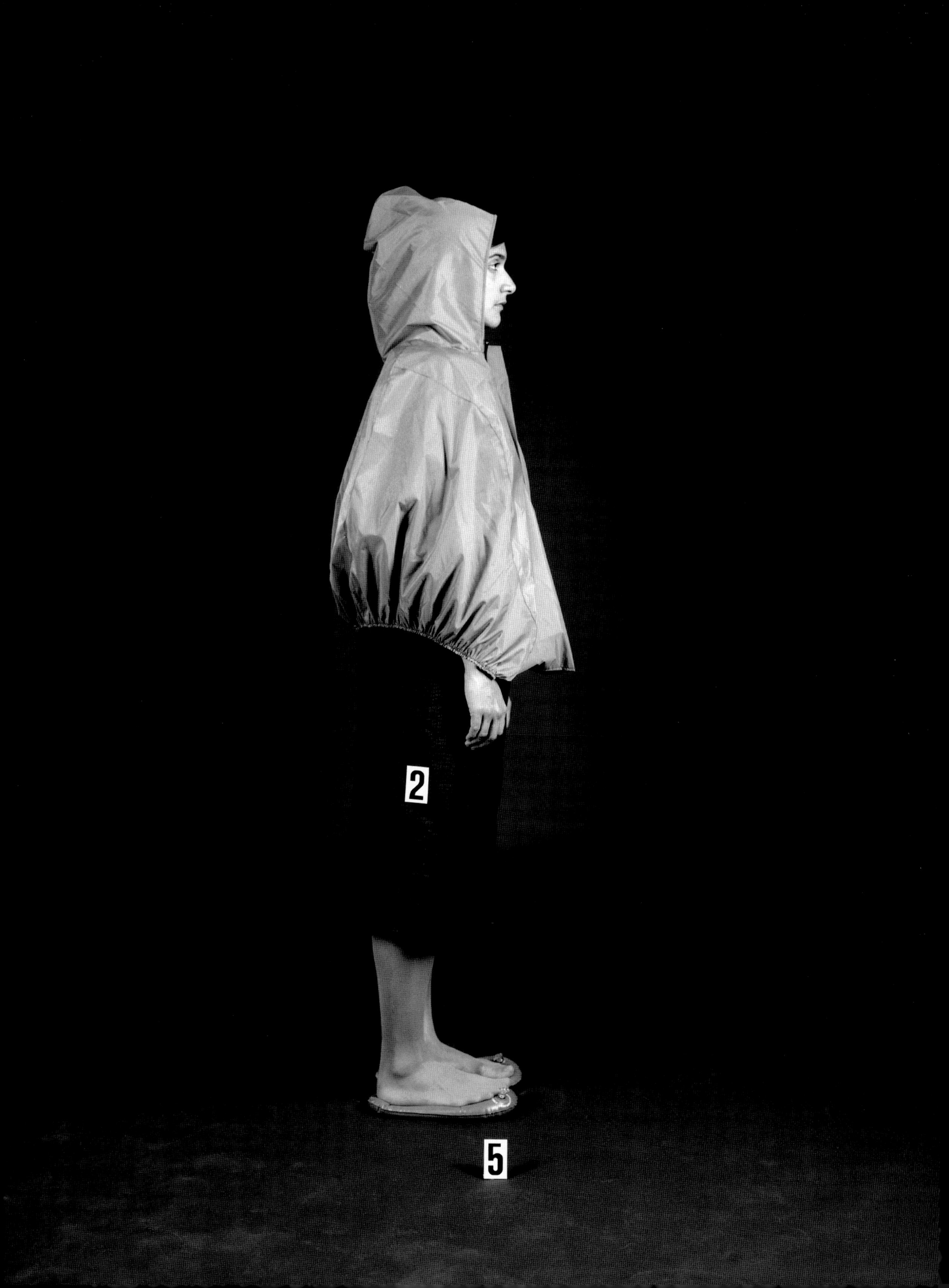
2
5

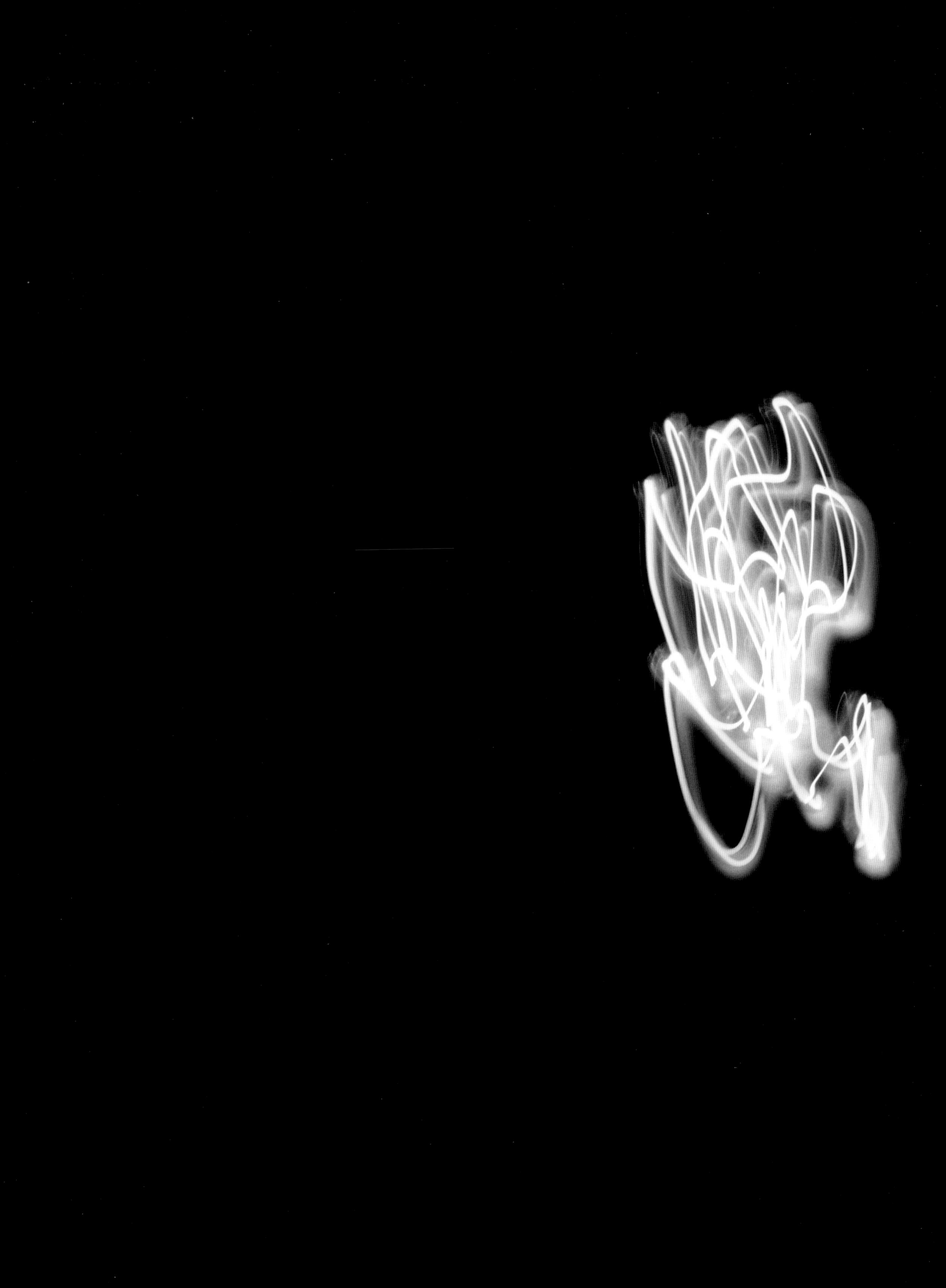

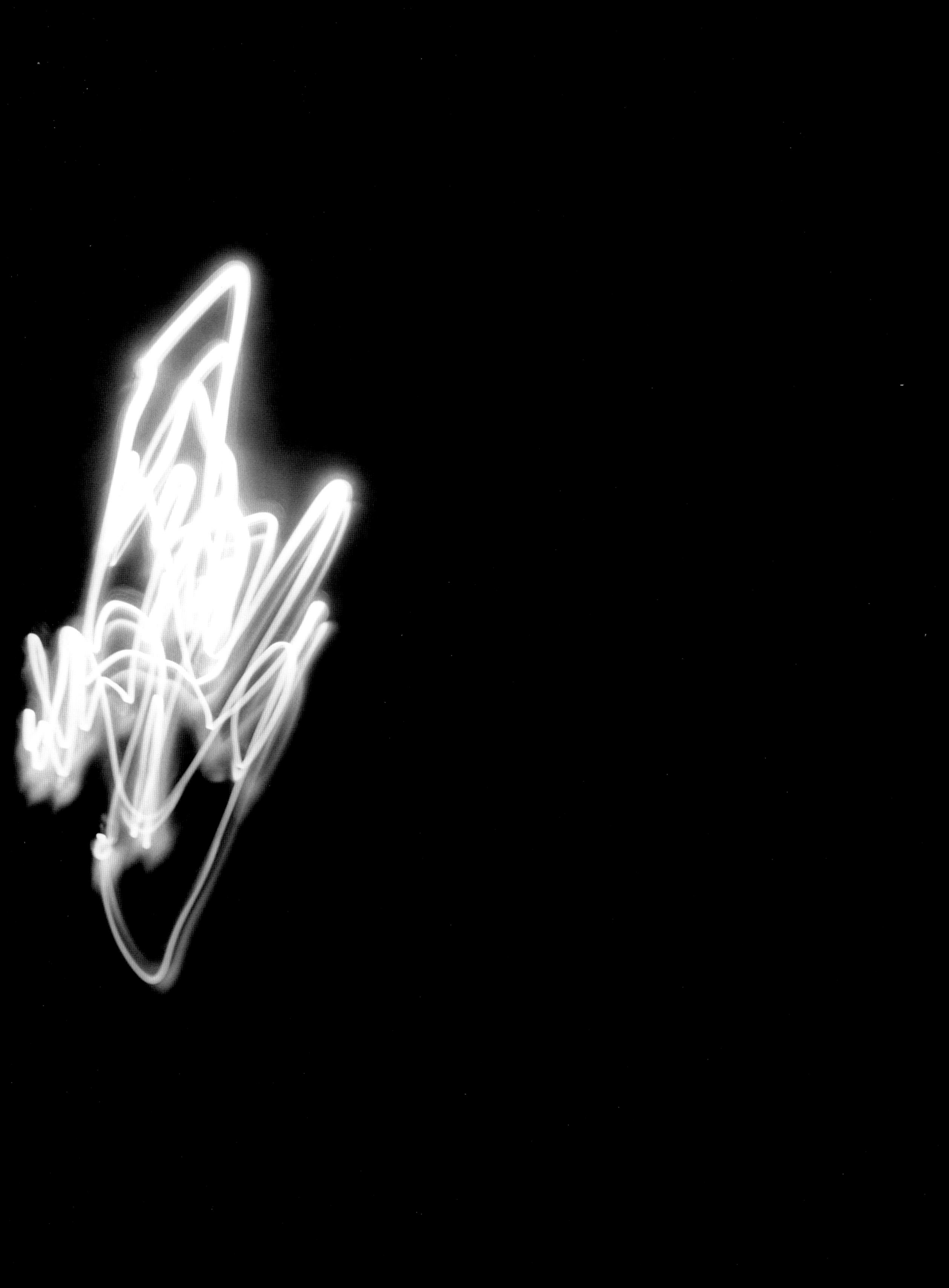

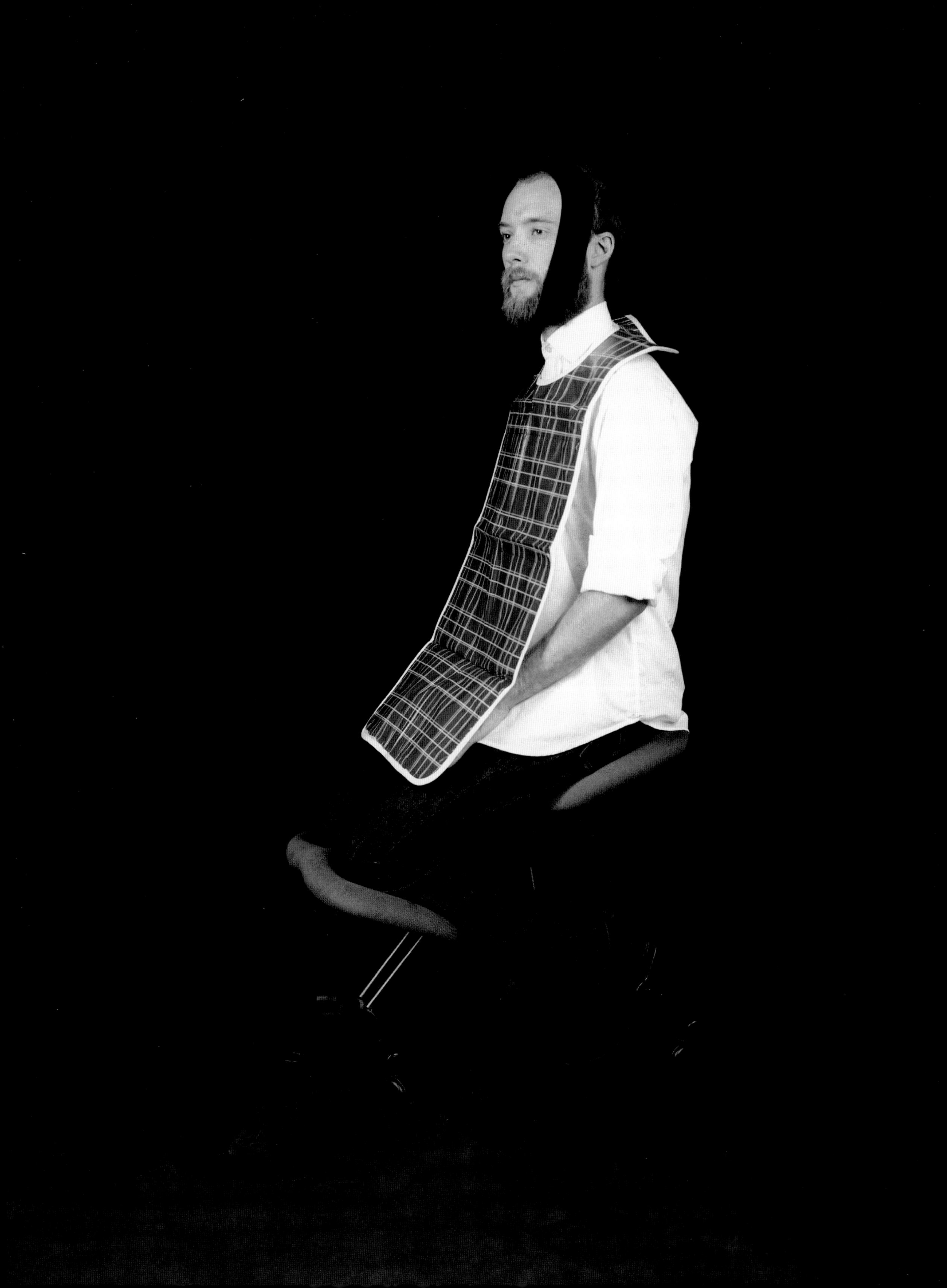

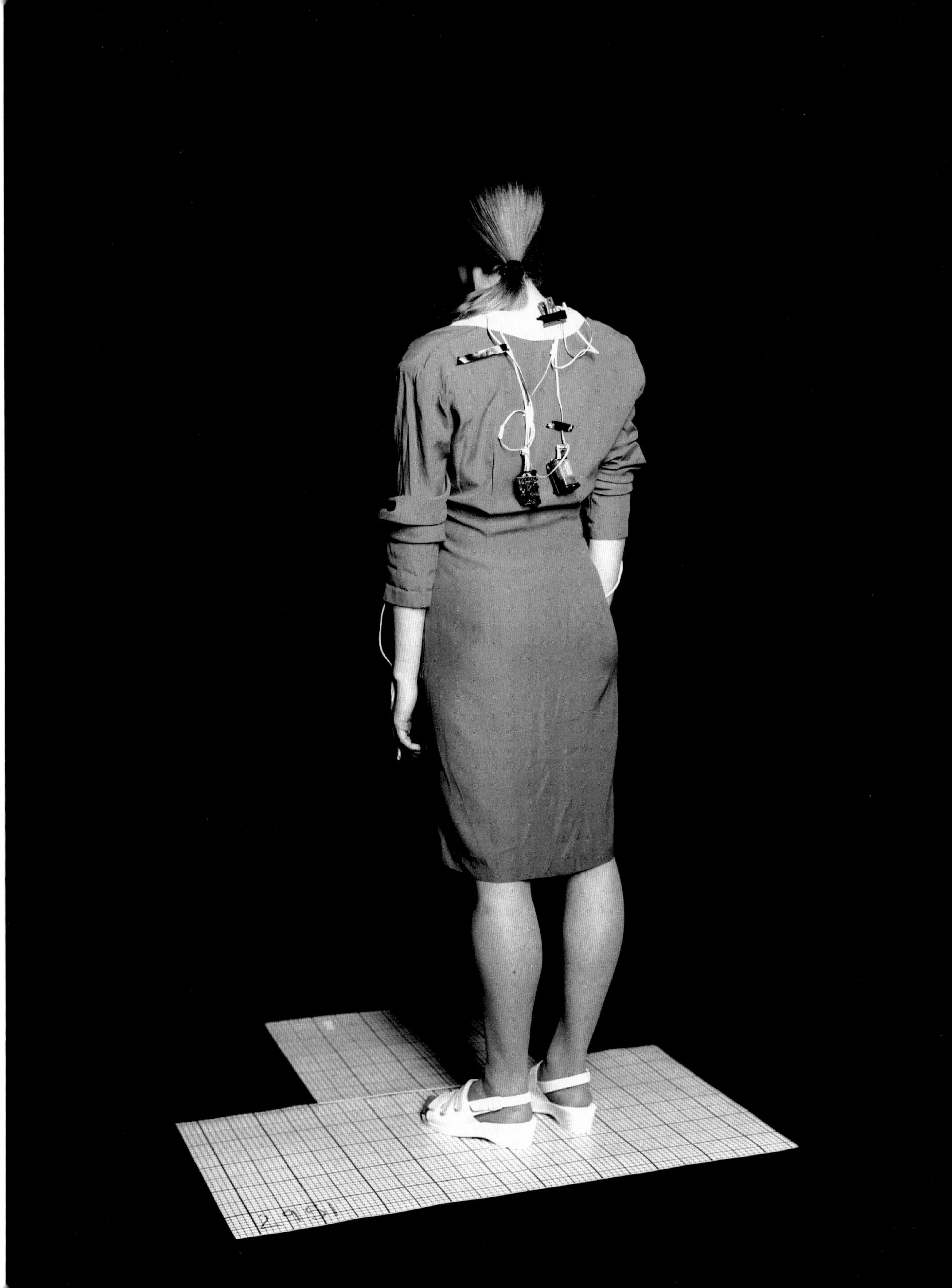

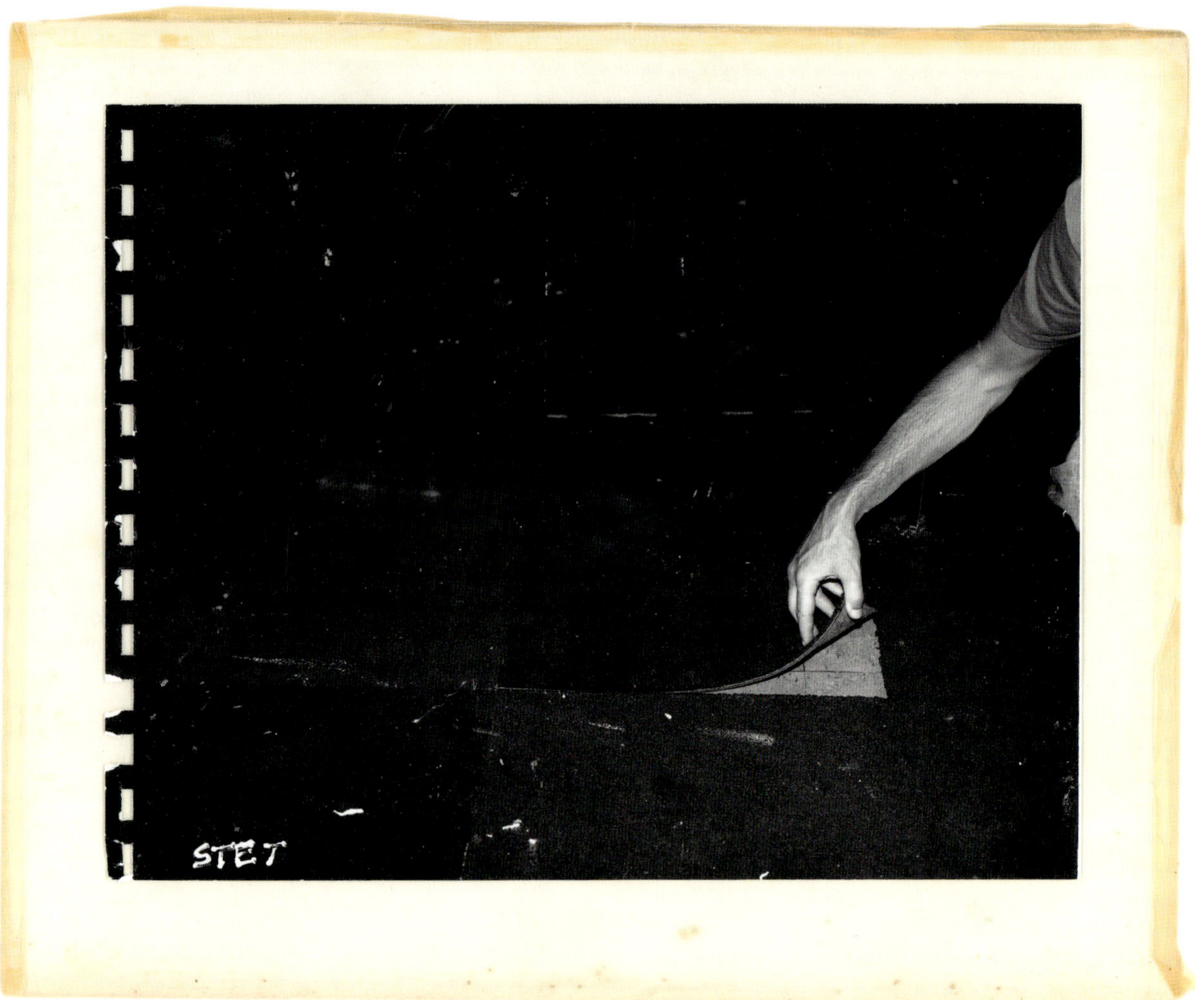
STET

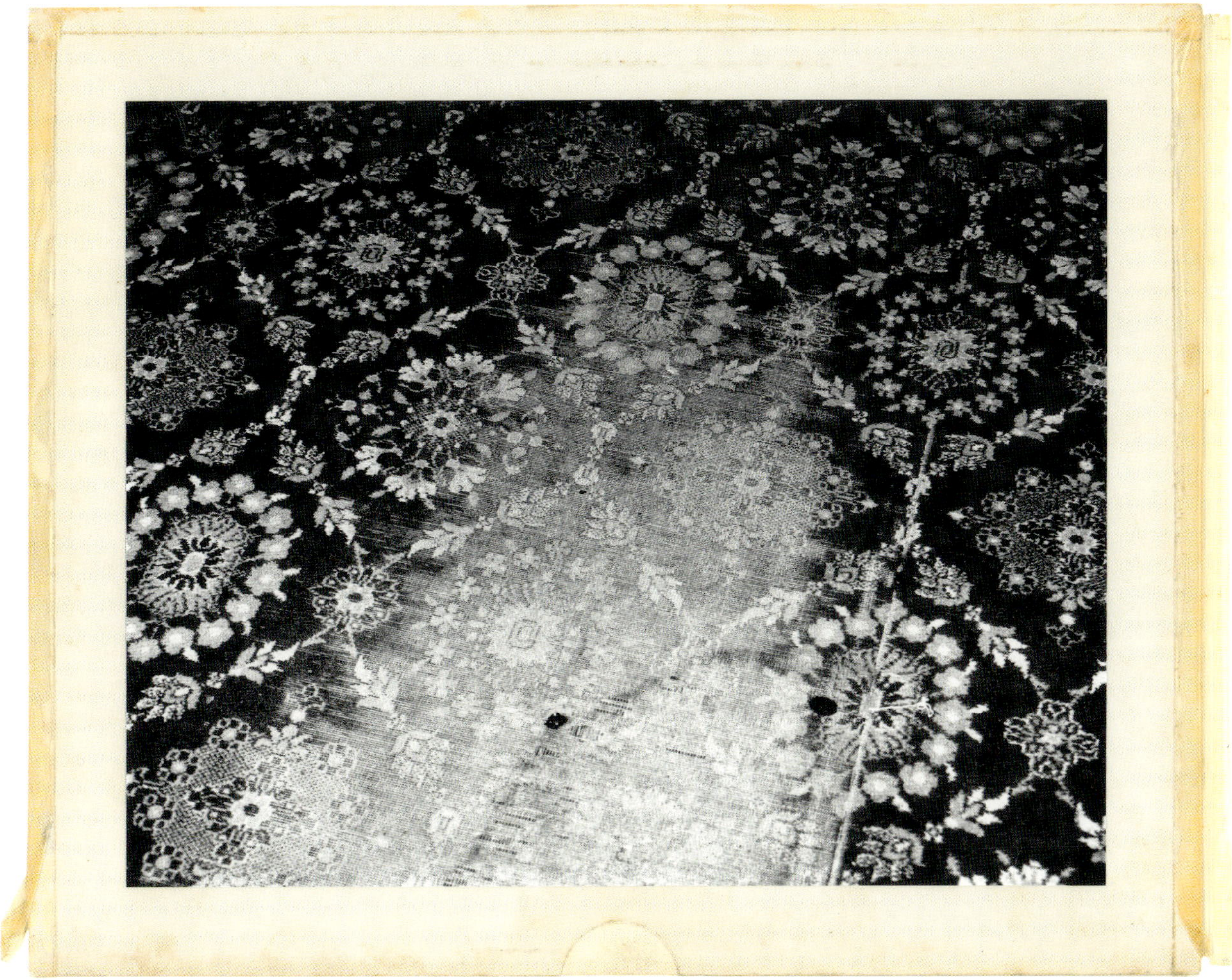

New Town Tales

An electricity meter reader alerted officials after reporting a putrid smell emanating from No.38 Broadgreen Estate. Further investigation led to the discovery of an unidentifiable body. From the telling signs of decomposition medical examiners estimated that the deceased had been dead for 7 weeks without detection.
News From Somewhere, 19th August 1966. (p28)

7.15am a black Volvo estate mounted the pavement and struck down an innocent pedestrian. The 73yr old woman sustained multiple injuries and was thought to have died instantaneously.
News From Somewhere, 27th January 1981. (p34)

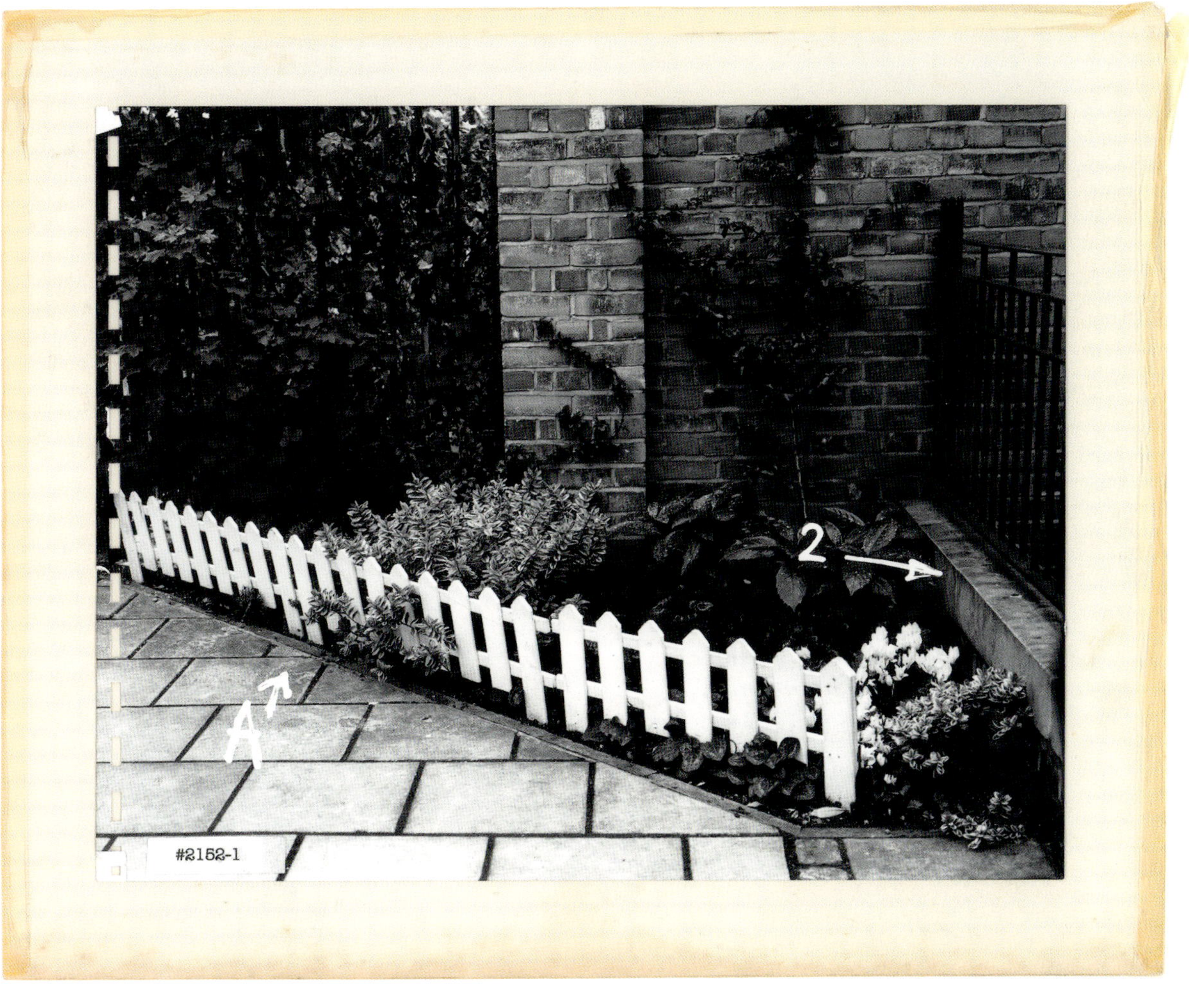
2
A
#2152-1

Investigators reported that location pattern analysis and trace evidence revealed that there were discrepancies between what was reported and what actually happened. Once the luminal compound reacted with the blood iron content the glow showed definite physical evidence of a cover up.
News From Somewhere, 1st September 1977. (p22)

Scene of Crime officers were called to the old industrial plant where a dog walker discovered a limbless torso concealed in a red gingham tablecloth. Police are mystified, as all identifiable markings had been removed from the corpse. Officials are now scouring the area for other body parts.
News From Somewhere, 23rd March 1979. (p2)

The teenager was last seen wearing a hooded red sweatshirt and white cotton trousers.
On the night of her disappearance she was seen laughing with friends at the local parade.
The 13 year old is reported to have run away on several occasions but has always returned.
She has now been missing for 17 days.
News From Somewhere, 11th April 2001. (p15)

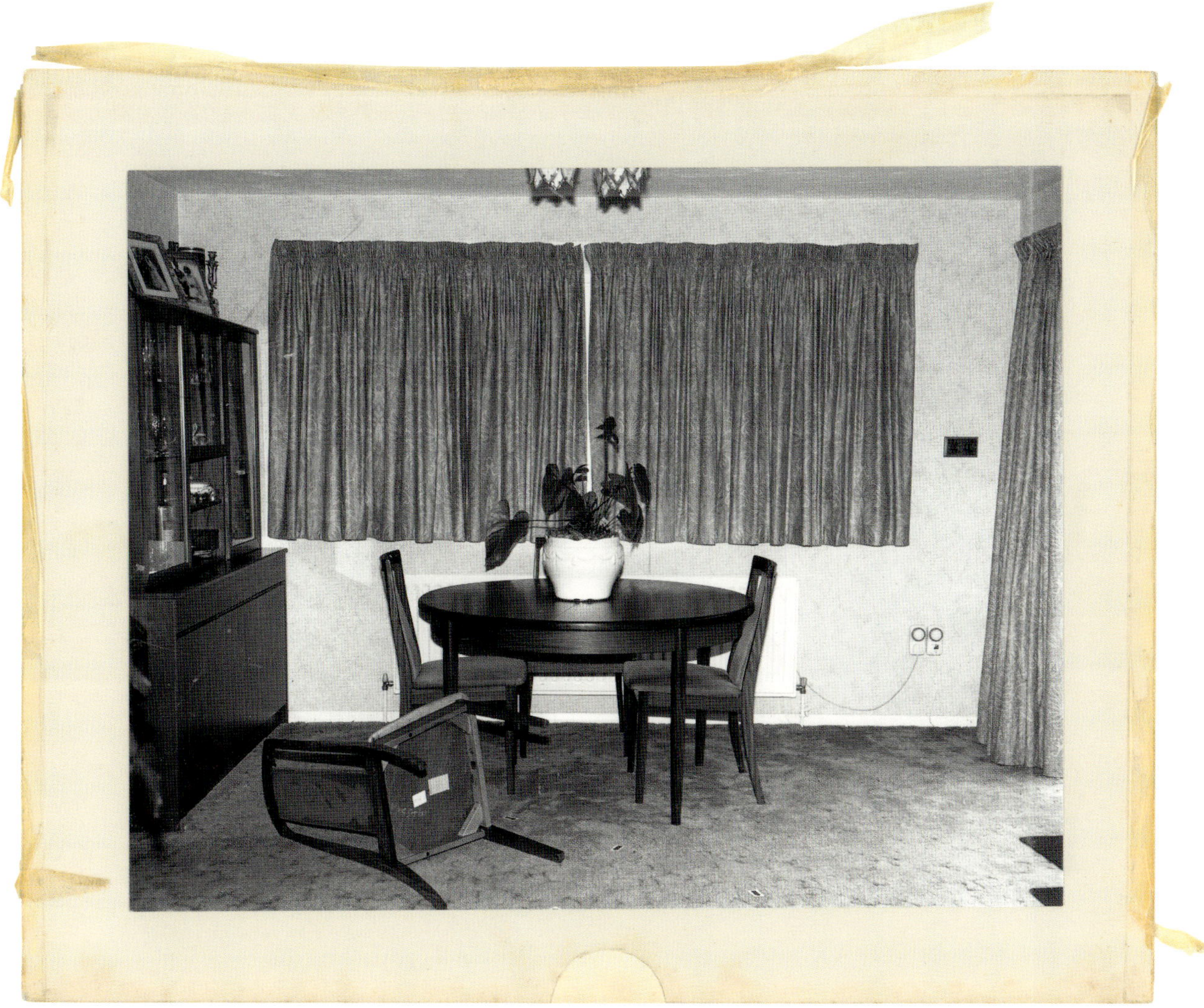

A young boy points to the spot where he uncovered a briefcase and brogues buried in local woodland. The attaché case contained a collection of season tickets with their photographs intact, a white stained shirt and a tie. The as yet undisclosed names have been entered into the system and all have been found on the missing persons register.
News From Somewhere, 15th August 1982. (p23)

Unusual stains were reported by estate agent Mrs A (identity withheld) after evaluating a vacant property in the area. The 3-bedroom end of terrace house was allegedly home to a young family who left the property some time last year. Concerned, Mrs A contacted authorities after finding "abnormal emissions" in the bath and on the bathroom walls.
News From Somewhere, 18th April 1987. (p12)

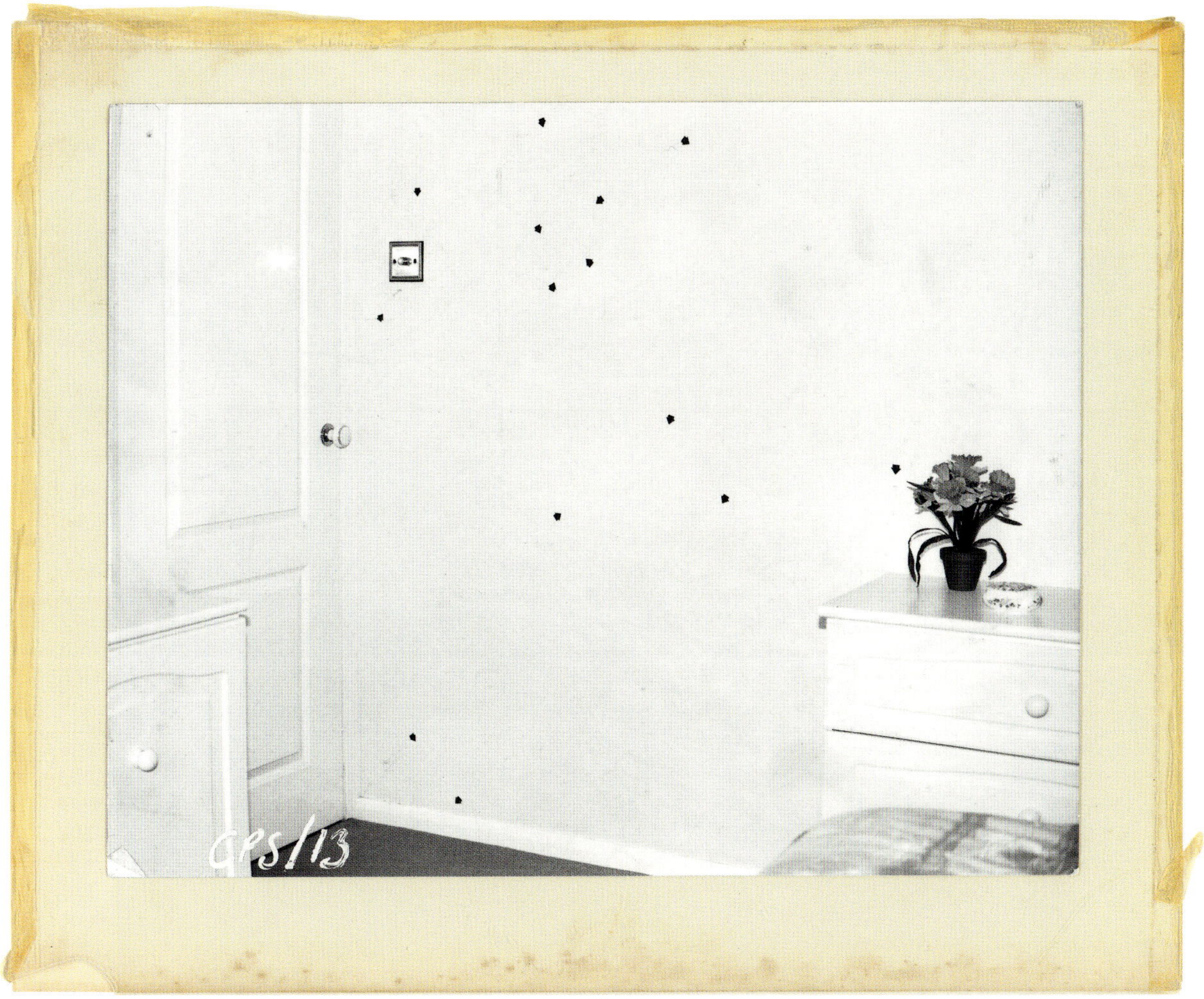
GPS/13

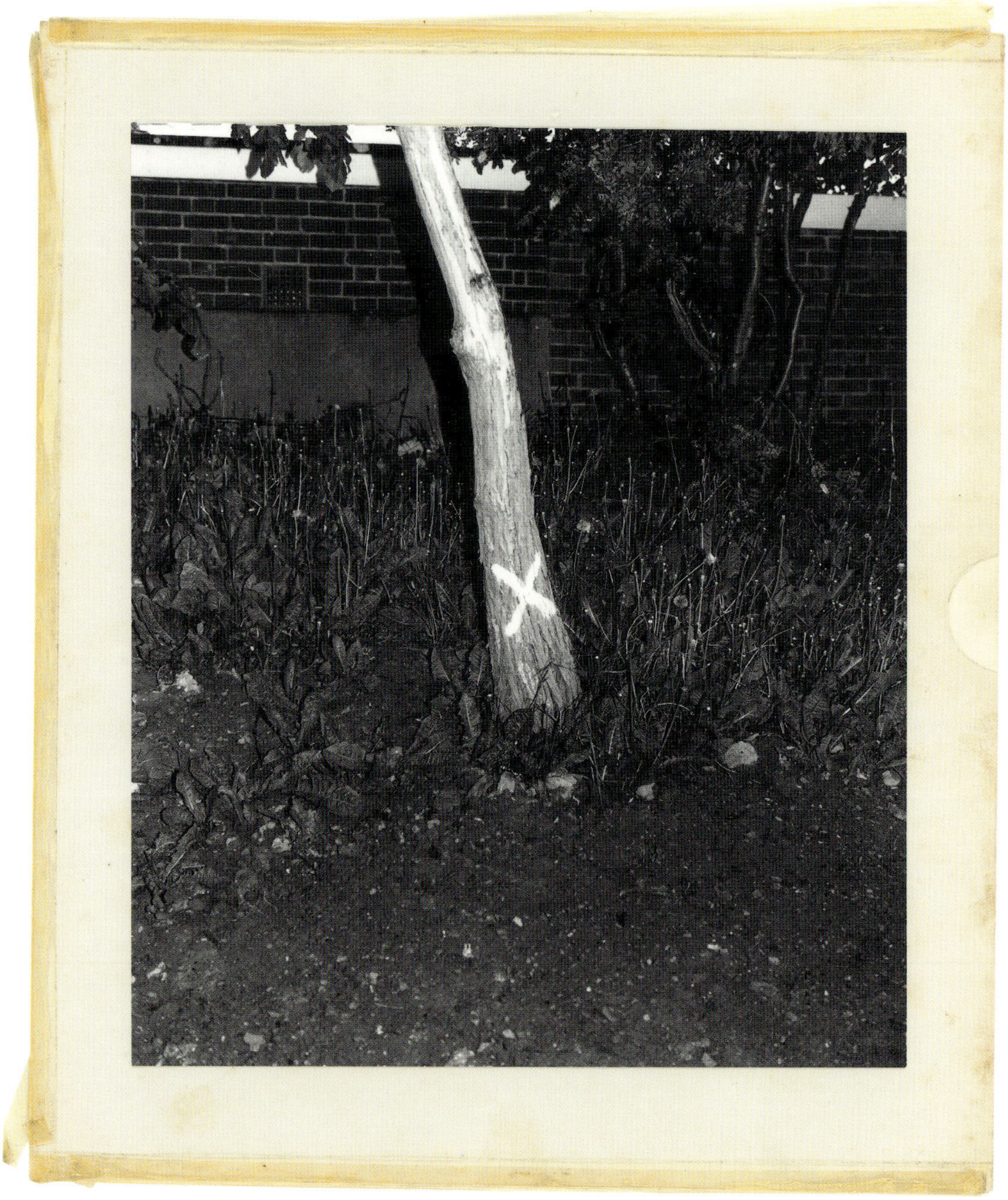

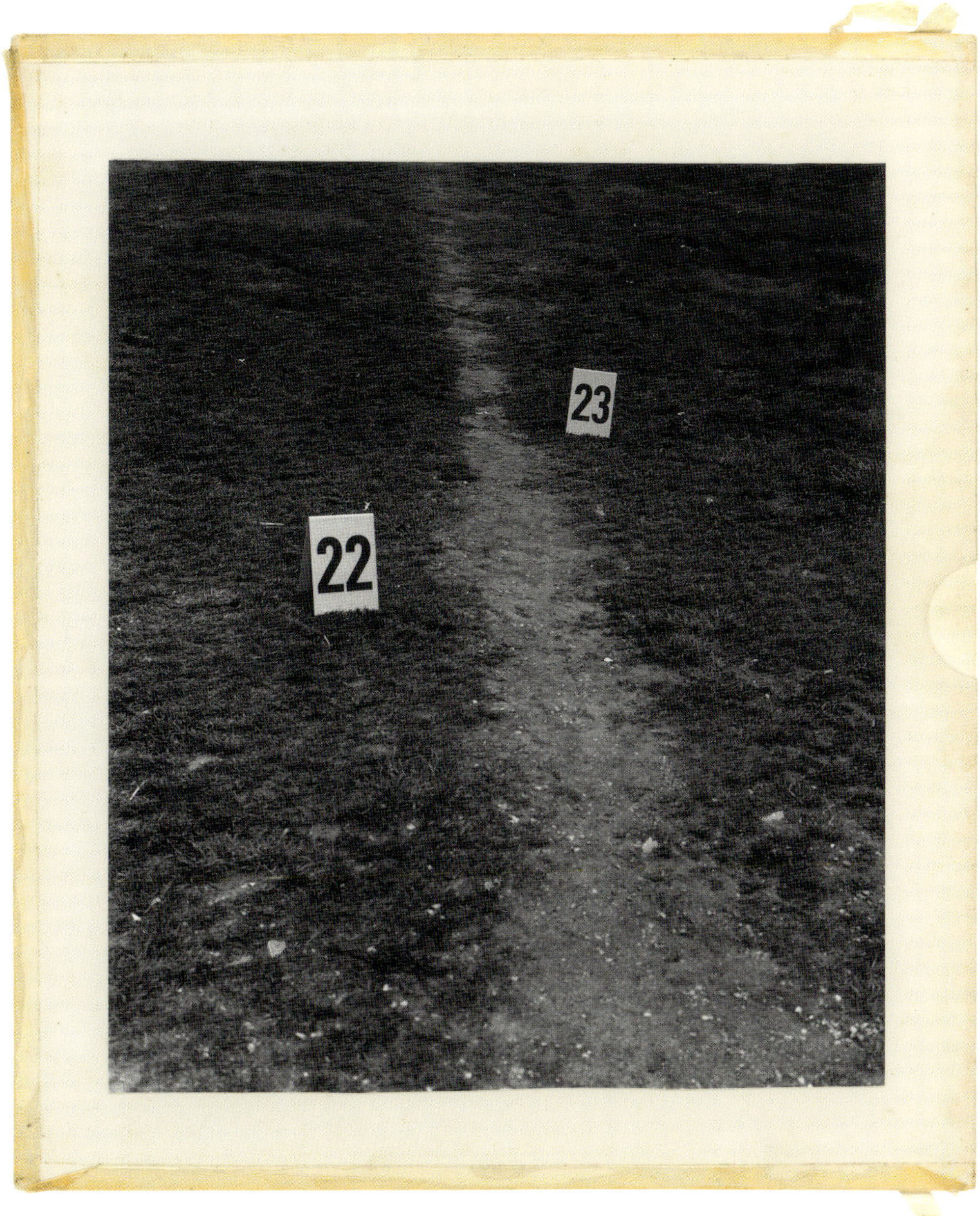
23
22

Citizens reported hearing screams in the middle of last night. The consensus suggests the cries originated from the town centre, "it sounded as if someone had been trapped and couldn't get out, I had to close all the windows" stated a fellow resident.
News From Somewhere, 12th January 1965. (p2)

A red BMW and a green Datsun collided yesterday. The driver of the BMW, a municipal civil servant, survived the impact, however all other occupants were found dead. Both cars are currently undergoing staged reconstruction as evidence has been pointing to mechanical foul play.
News From Somewhere, 28th February 1980. (p4)

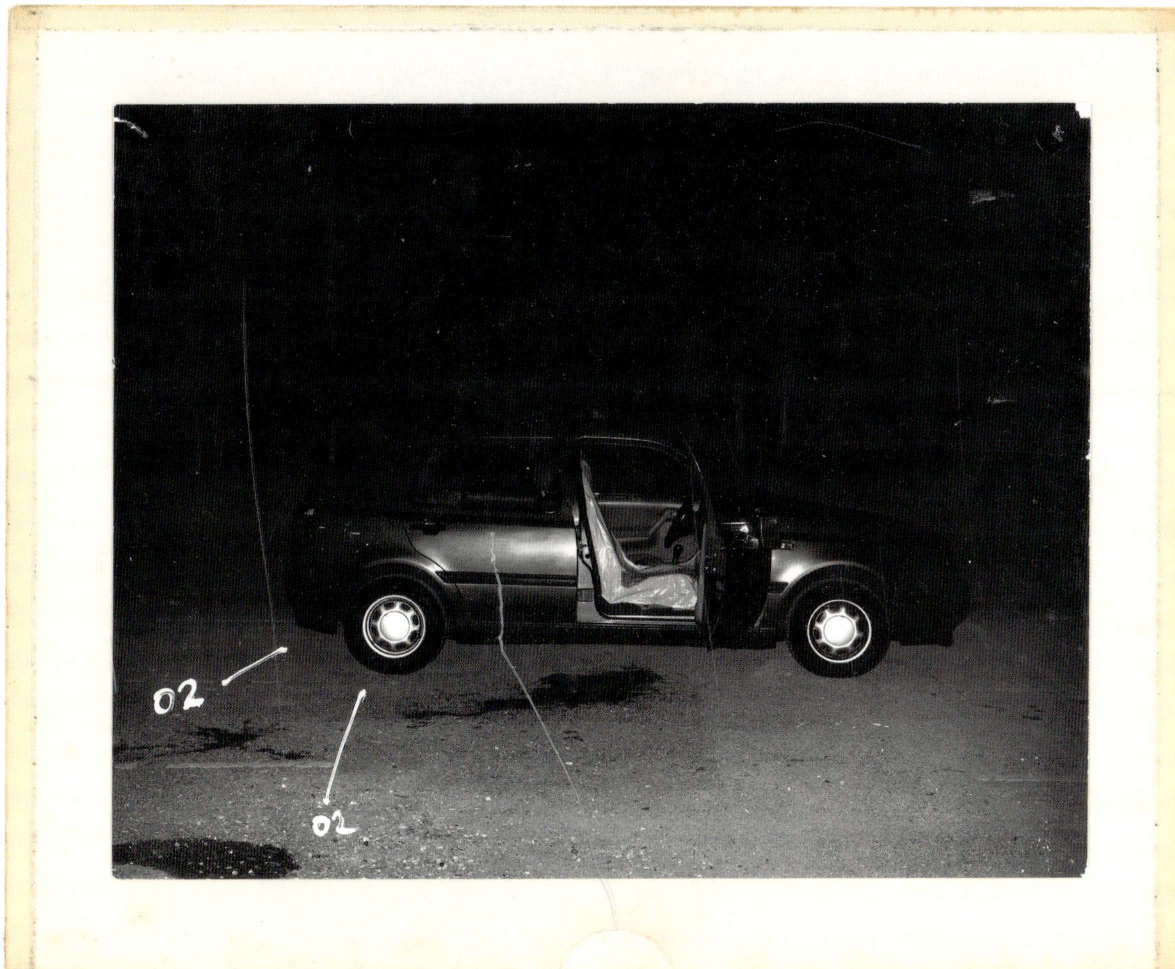
02
02

Unseen Agents

2006 – 2007

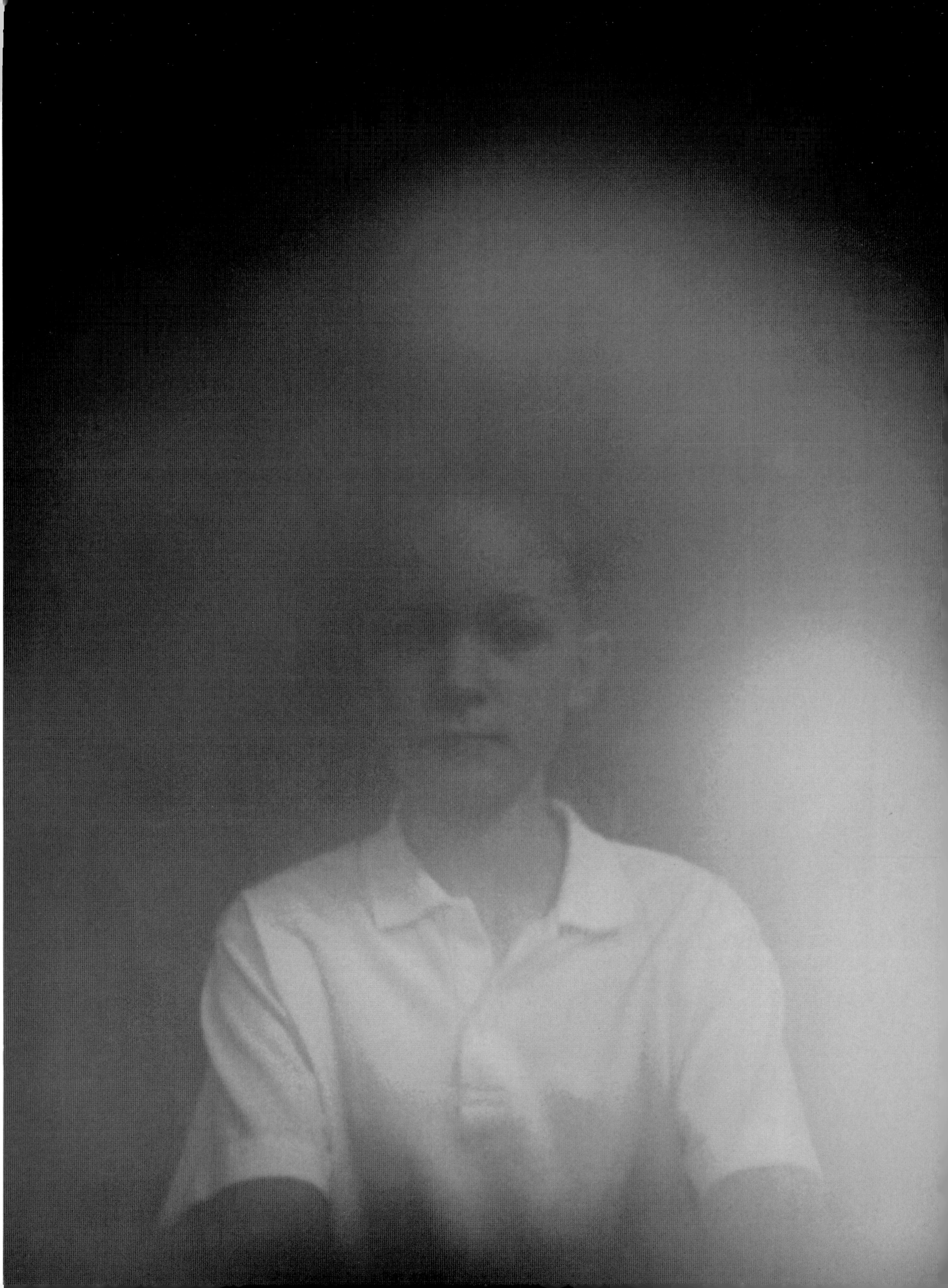

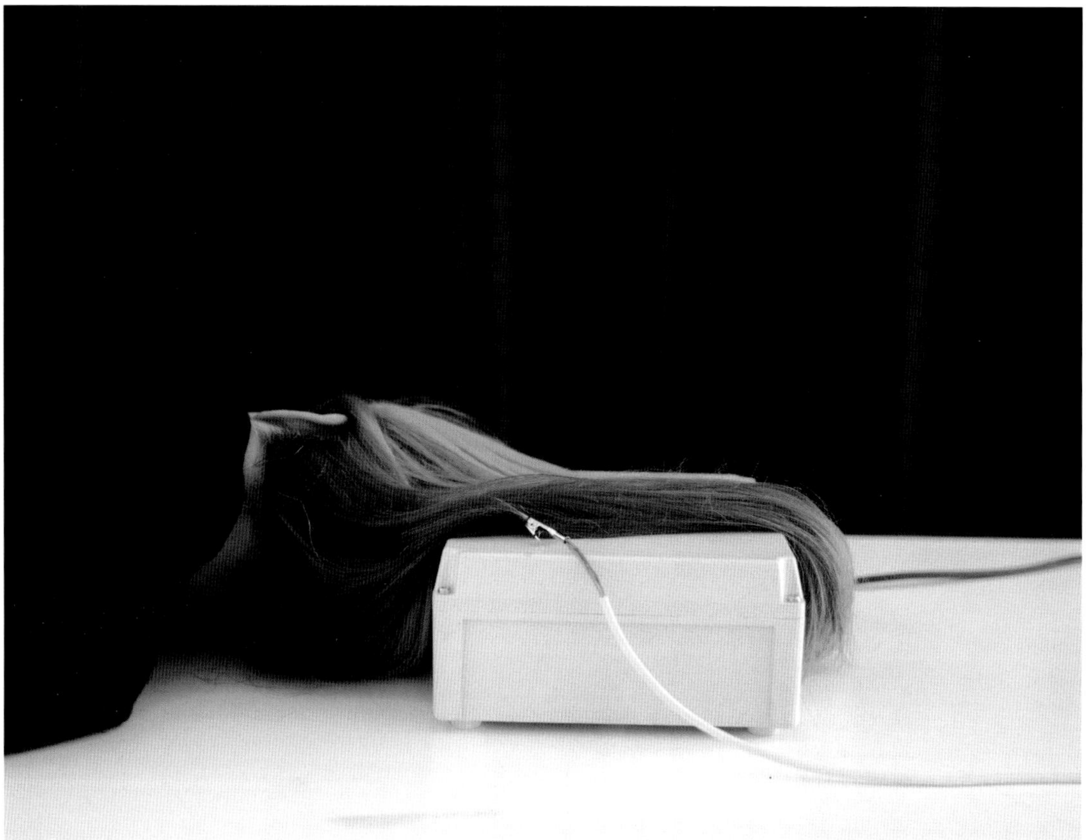

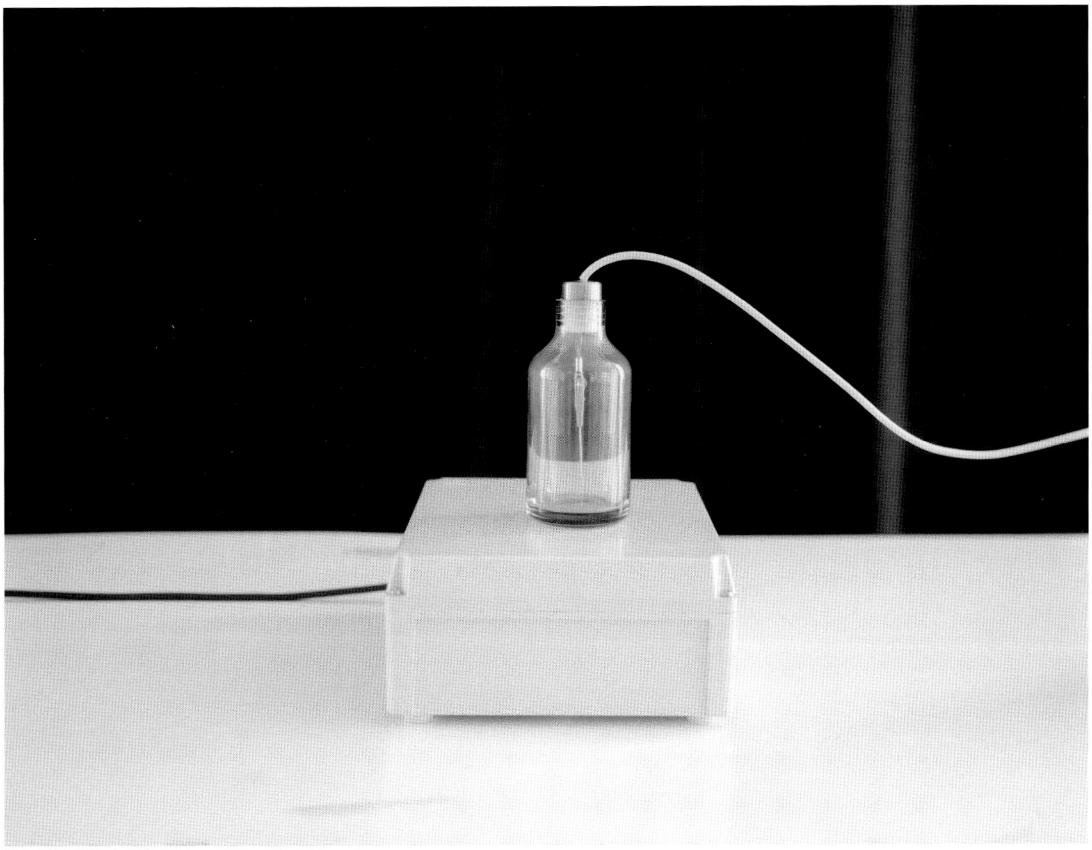

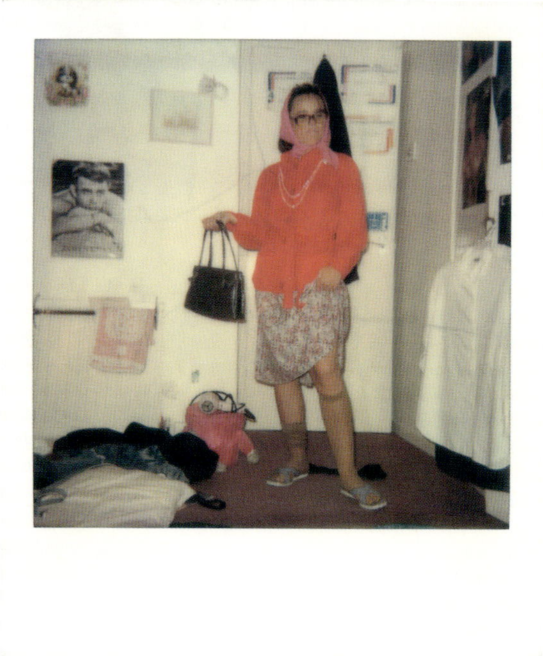

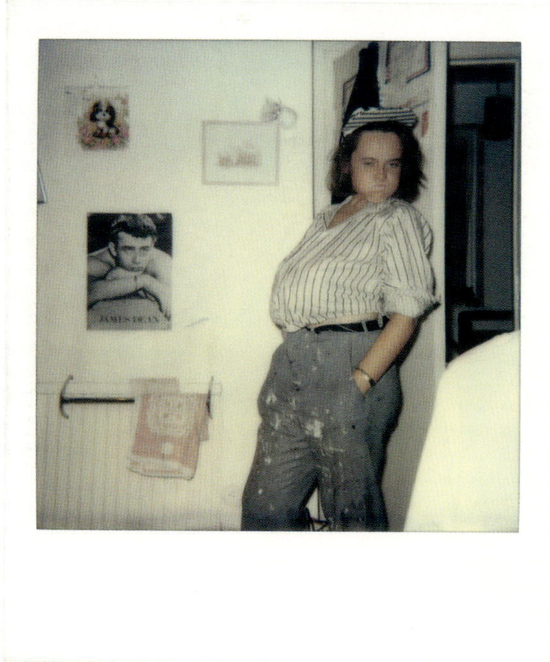
JAMES DEAN

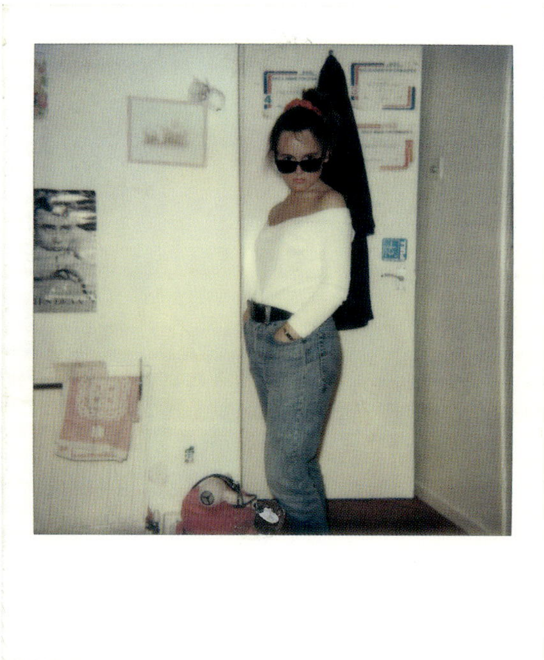

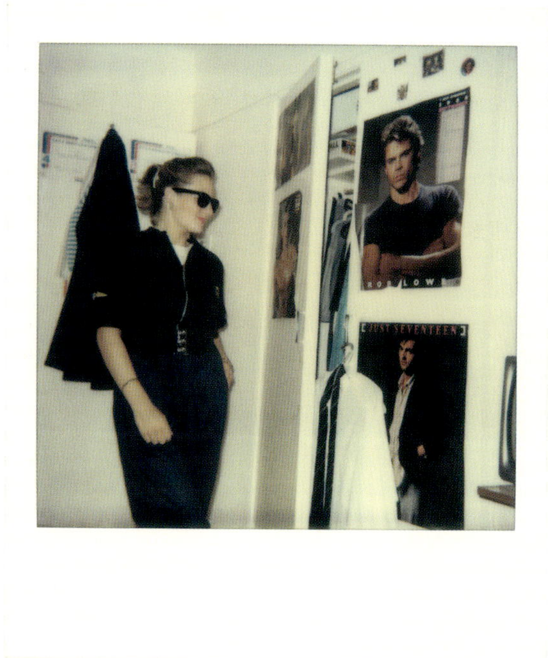
ROB LOWE
JUST SEVENTEEN

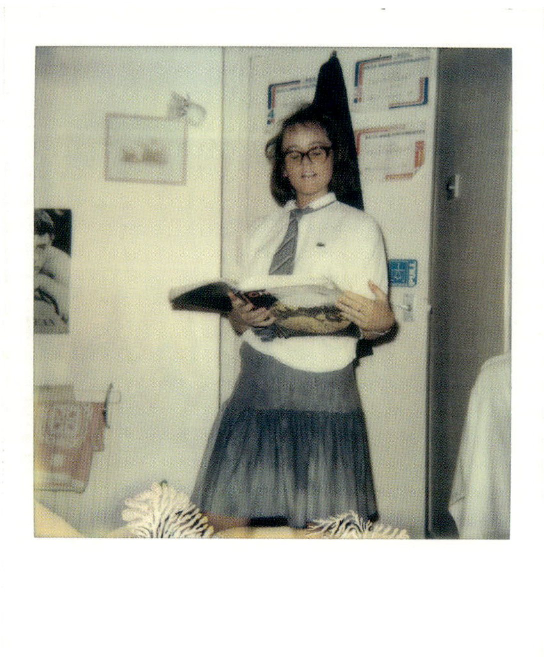

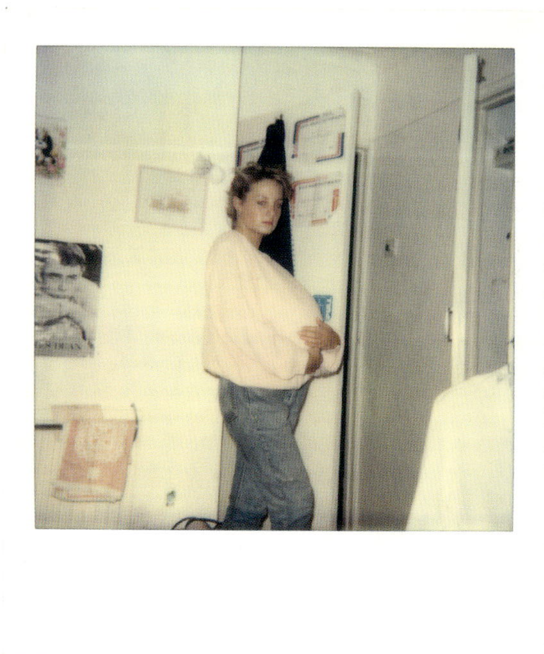

Interview

Clare Strand in conversation with Chris Mullen
Brighton, March 2008

Clare Strand and I have met regularly for many years to discuss her work and my own researches into photography. We have explored much common ground in identifying and celebrating utilitarian aspects of the medium. The interview for this book seemed an excellent opportunity to make an assessment of where she found herself as the first major collection of her visual work was published.

What sort of a photographer are you? Subject matter has always been the centre of my practice. I wouldn't bother if I didn't have a subject. I am not driven to take photographs for the sake of taking photographs. I take in information from my everyday life; it circulates and is refined before emerging as an idea for a project. Each piece of work determines what working methods I adopt, but the core elements of this process still remain.

I have a subject and when I determine its relationship to photography I start making work. I have always found it helpful to understand how I can use photography through an appreciation of utilitarian images. Consequently, all my work is about the nature of the medium of photography, its uses and its limitations. I like to operate within opposites – the extraordinary versus the ordinary, the factual as opposed to the unreal and the comedic offset by the serious.

In previous interviews you have stressed the importance of preparing yourself by exploring the context of a subject or proposition. Can you reflect on your attitude to the role that research plays in the photographic project? It's utterly serendipitous, I see something and seize it. It can come from anywhere. Then I take it to chew over. I am always looking around to see what could be brought into my work. I gather in all information then a section of it starts making sense to me. Not all research contributes to the outcome. It's more like throwing everything into a pot to see what rises to the top. It is an innate process for me and I like the sense of hidden order – and the sense of intuition and haphazardness.

I have a collection of images that I have kept with me from early on that consistently informs my practice. I have particular favourites such as the silhouettes of the murders carried out at the Tate residence by the Manson family. They are non-photographs – that's why I like them. There is something there that, even now, I don't particularly understand. There is a sort of uselessness in desperately trying to get photography to prove something. There is also a gap between the promise of these photographs and reality. It is, for me, also a type of absurdism.

Sometimes I get the feeling that some of your work reflects narratives from your past. What is your earliest memory? We were living in West Kingsdown, in a house in a cul-de-sac. There was a little girl I met who was older than me. She used to put sweets down her socks – those jelly snakes. When I was three we moved to Sanderstead, which was another house in a cul-de-sac. I'm really keen on the psychology of the cul-de-sac; going in, going round, and coming out again – all to no great purpose. Cul-de-sacs have an underlying notion of protection, unlike living on a main road where you are easily identified as being on a main route and you can't hide away.

What do you remember of that time, when you were the same age as many of the figures you now use in your work? Looking back I remember a distinctive, tangible sense of place – an identity and a taste almost. My school was set in woodland, we were always being told to watch out for danger and always to walk in pairs. It felt ominous. My street was also odd. There were individual inhabitants far beyond the ordinary – a flasher living directly opposite who would expose himself out of his bedroom window and a detective who once keenly showed me his collection of violent forensic photographs. He had a collection of images of a man who had committed suicide in his bathroom. The images were garish in colour with arterial spray on the walls and a body slumped in the corner. What struck me immediately was the intense clash of the extraordinary and the ordinary. The everyday paraphernalia of the bathroom was still intact – the shampoo, bubble bath and talc still lined up on the side of the bath. The towels were neatly hung up and the bathroom bin needed to be emptied. Something appalling had happened

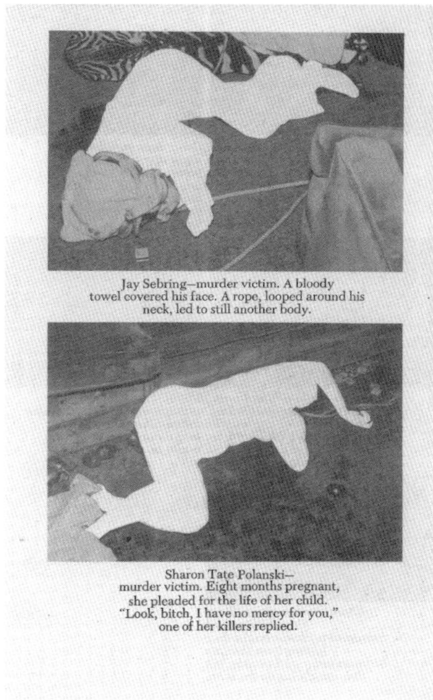

Crime – CR. 11. Manson Murders. Collection of Clare Strand.

Clare Strand and Lisa Akhurst, *Lisa's Bedroom, 1–6,* 1987 (Opposite)

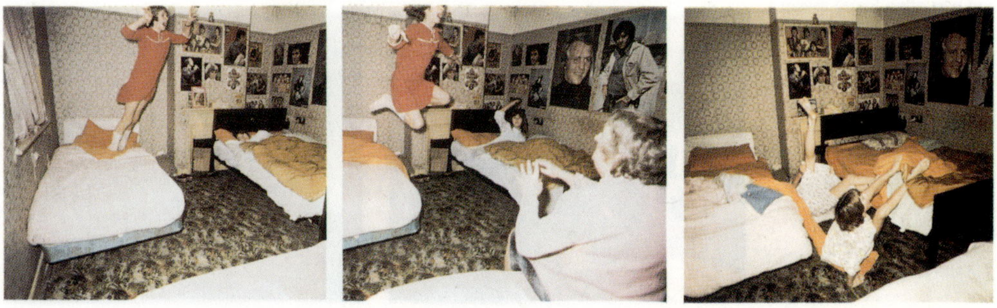

Paranormal – PA. 7. Enfield Poltergeist. Collection of Clare Strand.

and nothing would be the same again for those involved, but still the ordinariness of the everyday home remained to outlive its inhabitant. I think that this experience was behind *The Mortuary* work (1994–1995) where my focus was on the utensils and receptacles rather than on the individual. Again, I seek that middle ground between the extraordinary and the ordinary.

How did your interest in paranormal and crime photography come about? On my occasional visits to Sanderstead Library I would hone in on the paranormal and true crime section. There I learnt about young women like Mary Bell and Lizzie Borden, as well as the Enfield poltergeist manifestations as showcased in Arthur C Clarke's *World of Strange Powers*. I really do believe that what gets you in adolescent life remains with you forever. That's why I was keen to include the *Lisa's Bedroom* polaroids in this book, taken when I was about fourteen. I like the way they connect not only with my *Spice Girl* series (1996) and *Gone Astray Portraits* (2002–2003) but also the Enfield girls' bedroom.

You have spoken in the past about the significance of adolescent anxieties. In the light of your subsequent interests, were you yourself telekinetic, or prey to the supernatural? When I was in my early teens I experimented to try and move and levitate things – just in case I could, but nothing happened. I was utterly taken with the idea of girls being open to paranormal happenings – I also enjoyed reading about young women that had managed to fool investigative teams by banging on radiators or by voice manipulations. Films such as *The Watcher In The Wood*, *Carrie*, *The Exorcist*, *Fire Starter*, etc. all encouraged my early experiments. I also enjoyed reading the *Fortean Times* and watching *Record Breakers* (in particular the girl who held the record for not being able to stop sneezing), and Ripley's *Believe it or Not*.

I have sometimes teased you about a suspected fear of colour photography. What choices do you make when you select black and white photography? After graduating from the Royal College of Art, I started making work in black and white, in reaction to the photographic climate of the time. Colour work started to make me feel claustrophobic – it was too busy and I felt the need to find a new working space. Using black and white offers me clarity. It also brings me nearer to the utilitarian images I admire the most. For me, black and white strips down the elements – it helps me be more decisive and offers the drama/non-drama and the ambiguity I am looking for in an image.

Gone Astray *was a major threshold for you. I always thought it was a sign that you were taking this medium seriously as a mode of expression for the future.* *Gone Astray* was the culmination of a year's fellowship at the London College of Printing (now LCC). I took this as an opportunity to research certain aspects of the City. I was intrigued by urban critics, such as Dickens (whose essay of 1853 on his being lost as a child in the City, gave the project its name), William Morris and William Blake. But it was Henry Mayhew's small text about street

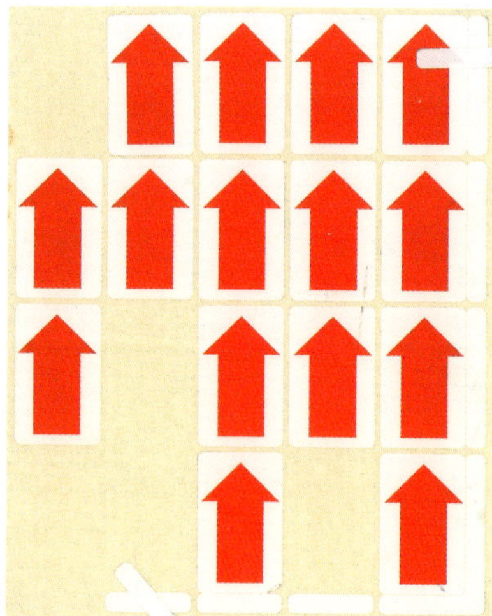

Forensic Arrow Collection – 1/25. Collection of Clare Strand.

photographers in *London Labour and the London Poor*, where he talks about photographers using the painted circus tents as material for backdrops, that helped to start form the idea for the *Portraits*. I was also keen to explore the relationship and tensions between the countryside and the city.

Yet I sense the subject matter of the project contains elements beyond the tangible, and doesn't exactly seek to exert a social critique. Is that so? I was walking in Clerkenwell and a woman suddenly fell to her knees, as if brought low by some hidden subterranean force. It alerted me to what was happening underneath the hum of the pavement, the tunnels and channels – what is there and what is not there? I followed ideas of magic and the supernatural in the City, such as Peter Ackroyd's *The House of Doctor Dee* (1993) and above all, *Hawksmoor* (1986). It was a fusion of intuition, observation and reading that allowed *Gone Astray Details* to emerge, filtering conventional research through my own experiences via the photographic language of the instructional combined with the documentary.

The individual portraits express what you have called a 'general characterisation'. What do you mean by this? Each character is a constructed 'type', cast as you would actors, with similarly carefully selected props. They are types of people I would expect to find on any urban street. If they weren't there, I'd want to know why not. That is why I used the Dickens quote from *Gone Astray* as he talks about double lives, about people pretending, colluding with the theatrical element of the street. Many times I have moments wondering if people have been placed on the streets from central casting – as their being there is too expected, too clichéd. I am also interested in the small clues such as a Tiffany necklace or a teenage stoop that can express prowess or status.

Do your images do things you never anticipated after they are first shown? I'm always working to my own set of rules. Some rules are more obvious than others. After the images are made, you let them go into the world and, after that,

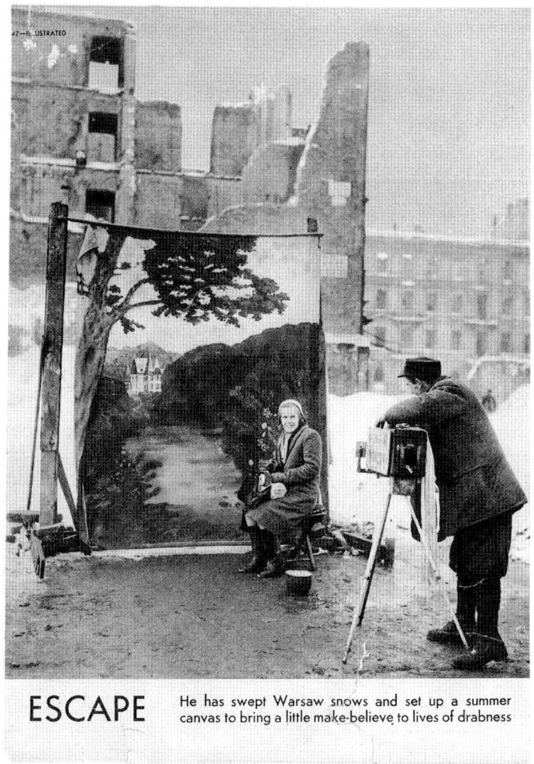

Gone Astray – GA. 7.
Collection of Clare Strand.

I have little idea of what people make of them. I enjoy following the clues of a mystery, but when the mysteries appear solved, the image becomes less and less interesting to me. The question is always 'how much to give away to the viewer?' It is possible to explain the image away and allow viewers no space for their own interpretation. Even now, there are issues throughout my work that I want to leave 'unsolved'.

***Can you talk about how this relates to* Signs of a Struggle?** *Signs of a Struggle* was a commissioned response to the New Town concept on its 50th anniversary. I started the project by asking what New Towns meant to me in particular. I wanted to leave the frame of reference open. The final images were either contemporary constructions of invented narratives or, alternatively, authentic images discovered in their folders in an archive. The work is about Utopia, the problems of idealism and imperfection. It is a commission, like most

Markings On Photographs – M. 23-58.
Collection of Clare Strand.

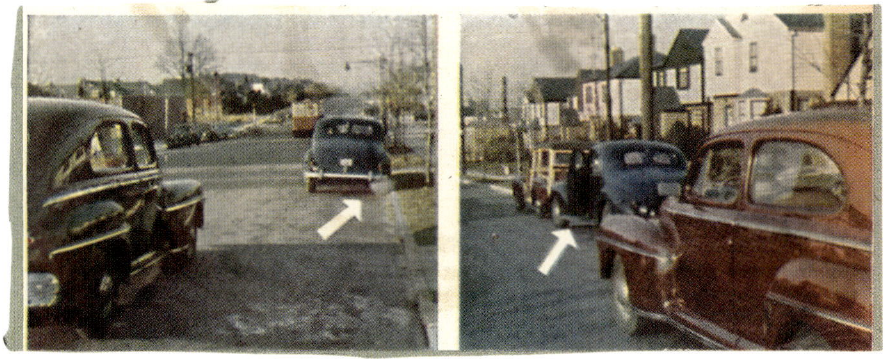

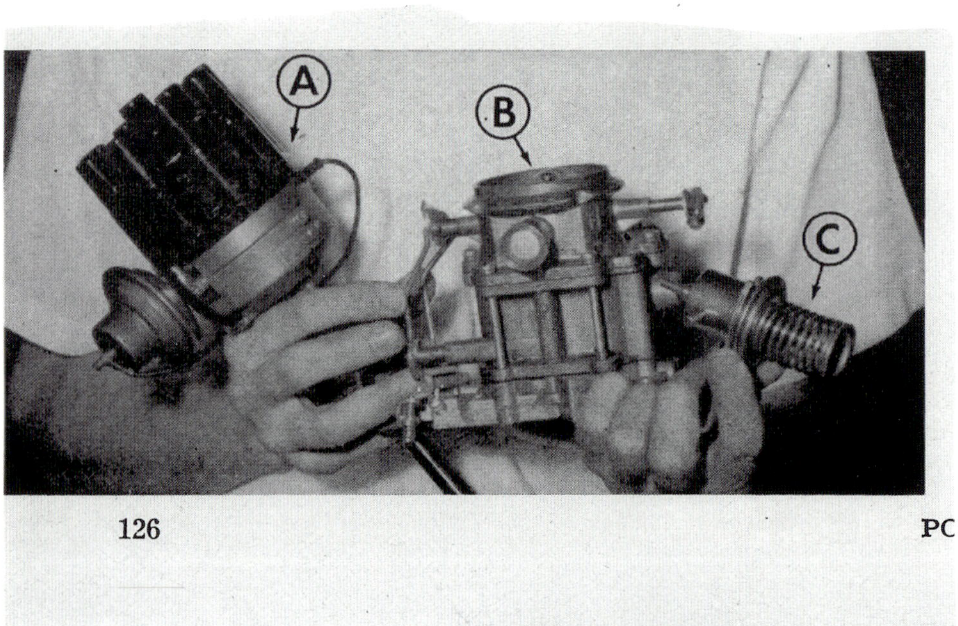

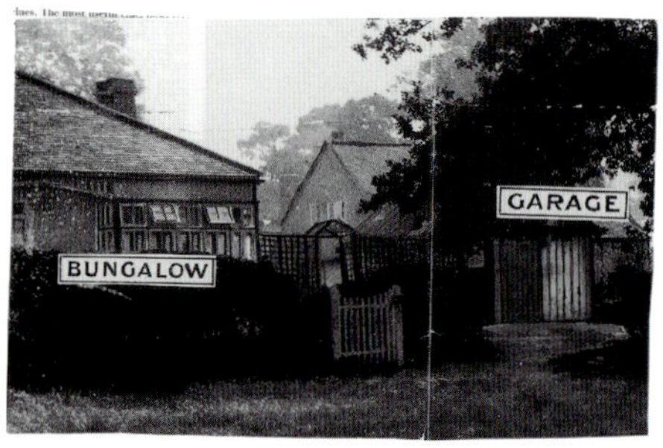

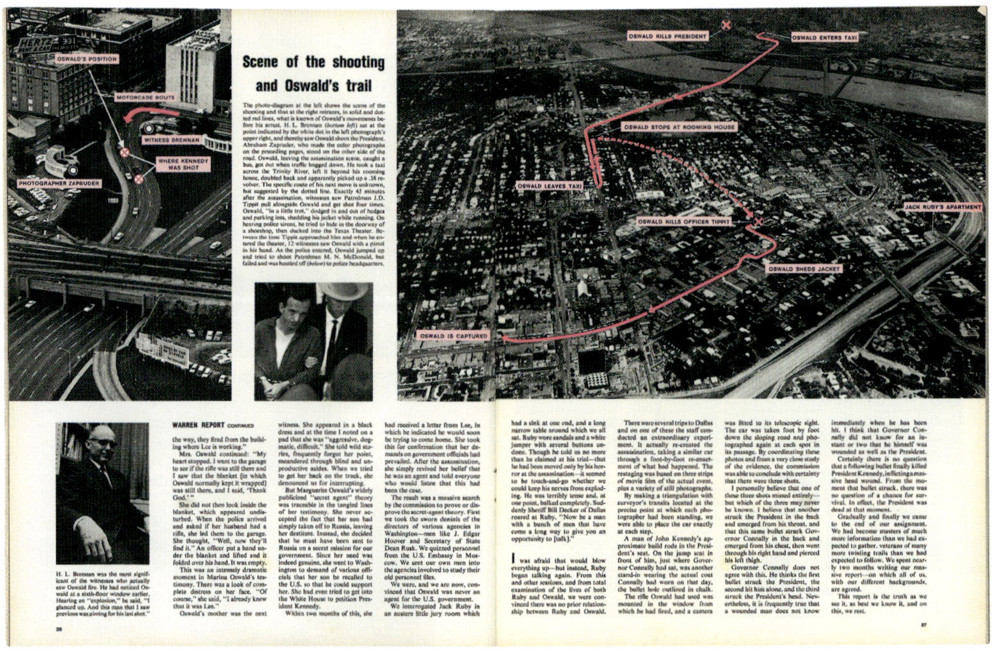

Scene of the shooting and Oswald's trail

The photo-diagram at the left shows the scene of the shooting and that at the right retraces, in solid and dotted red lines, what is known of Oswald's movements before his arrest. H. L. Brennan (*bottom left*) sat at the point indicated by the white dot in the left photograph's upper right, and thereby saw Oswald shoot the President. Abraham Zapruder, who made the color photographs on the preceding pages, stood on the other side of the road. Oswald, leaving the assassination scene, caught a bus, got out when traffic bogged down. He took a taxi across the Trinity River, left it beyond his rooming house, doubled back and apparently picked up a .38 revolver. The specific route of his next move is unknown, but suggested by the dotted line. Exactly 45 minutes after the assassination, witnesses saw Patrolman J.D. Tippit pull alongside Oswald and get shot four times. Oswald, "in a little trot," dodged in and out of hedges and parking lots, shedding his jacket while running. On hearing police sirens, he tried to hide in the doorway of a shoeshop, then ducked into the Texas Theater. Between the time Tippit approached him and when he entered the theater, 12 witnesses saw Oswald with a pistol in his hand. As the police entered, Oswald jumped up and tried to shoot Patrolman M. N. McDonald, but failed and was hustled off (*below*) to police headquarters.

H. L. Brennan was the most significant of the witnesses who actually saw Oswald fire. He had noticed Oswald at a sixth-floor window earlier. Hearing an "explosion," he said, "I glanced up. And this man that I saw previous was aiming for his last shot."

WARREN REPORT CONTINUED

the way, they fired from the building where Lee is working."

Mrs. Oswald continued: "My heart stopped. I went to the garage to see if the rifle was still there and I saw that the blanket [in which Oswald normally kept it wrapped] was still there, and I said, 'Thank God.'"

She did not then look inside the blanket, which appeared undisturbed. When the police arrived and asked if her husband had a rifle, she led them to the garage. She thought, "Well, now they'll find it." An officer put a hand under the blanket and lifted and it folded over his hand. It was empty.

This was an intensely dramatic moment in Marina Oswald's testimony. There was a look of complete distress on her face. "Of course," she said, "I already knew that it was Lee."

Oswald's mother was the next witness. She appeared in a black dress and at the time I noted on a pad that she was "aggressive, dogmatic, difficult." She told wild stories, frequently forgot her point, meandered through blind and unproductive asides. When we tried to get her back on the track, she denounced us for interrupting.

But Marguerite Oswald's widely publicized "secret agent" theory was traceable in the tangled lines of her testimony. She never accepted the fact that her son had simply taken off to Russia, leaving her destitute. Instead, she decided that he must have been sent to Russia on a secret mission for our government. Since her need was indeed genuine, she went to Washington to demand of various officials that her son be recalled to the U.S. so that he could support her. She had even tried to get into the White House to petition President Kennedy.

Within two months of this, she had received a letter from Lee, in which he indicated he would soon be trying to come home. She took this for confirmation that her demands on government officials had prevailed. After the assassination, she simply revived her belief that he was an agent and told everyone who would listen that this had been the case.

The result was a massive search by the commission to prove or disprove the secret-agent theory. First we took the sworn denials of the directors of various agencies in Washington—men like J. Edgar Hoover and Secretary of State Dean Rusk. We quizzed personnel from the U.S. Embassy in Moscow. We sent our own men into the agencies involved to study their old personnel files.

We were, and we are now, convinced that Oswald was never an agent for the U.S. government.

We interrogated Jack Ruby in an austere little jury room which had a sink at one end, and a long narrow table around which we all sat. Ruby wore sandals and a white jumper with several buttons undone. Though he told us no more than he claimed at his trial—that he had been moved only by his horror at the assassination—it seemed to be touch-and-go whether we could keep his nerves from exploding. He was terribly tense and, at one point, balked completely. Suddenly Sheriff Bill Decker of Dallas roared at Ruby. "Now be a man with a bunch of men that have come a long way to give you an opportunity to [talk]."

I was afraid that would blow everything up—but instead, Ruby began talking again. From this and other sessions, and from total examination of the lives of both Ruby and Oswald, we were convinced there was no prior relationship between Ruby and Oswald.

There were several trips to Dallas and on one of these the staff conducted an extraordinary experiment. It actually re-created the assassination, taking a similar car through a foot-by-foot re-enactment of what had happened. The restaging was based on three strips of movie film of the actual event, plus a variety of still photographs.

By making a triangulation with surveyor's transits located at the precise point at which each photographer had been standing, we were able to place the car exactly at each step.

A man of John Kennedy's approximate build rode in the President's seat. On the jump seat in front of him, just where Governor Connally had sat, was another stand-in wearing the actual coat Connally had worn on that day, the bullet hole outlined in chalk.

The rifle Oswald had used was mounted in the window from which he had fired, and a camera was fitted to its telescopic sight. The car was taken foot by foot down the sloping road and photographed again at each spot in its passage. By coordinating these photos and from a very close study of the evidence, the commission was able to conclude with certainty that there were three shots.

I personally believe that one of these three shots missed entirely—but which of the three may never be known. I believe that another struck the President in the back and emerged from his throat, and that this same bullet struck Governor Connally in the back and emerged from his chest, then went through his right hand and pierced his left thigh.

Governor Connally does not agree with this. He thinks the first bullet struck the President, the second hit him alone, and the third struck the President's head. Nevertheless, it is frequently true that a wounded man does not know immediately when he has been hit. I think that Governor Connally did not know for an instant or two that he himself was wounded as well as the President.

Certainly there is no question that a following bullet finally killed President Kennedy, inflicting a massive head wound. From the moment that bullet struck, there was no question of a chance for survival. In effect, the President was dead at that moment.

Gradually and finally we came to the end of our assignment. We had become masters of much more information than we had expected to gather, veterans of many more twisting trails than we had expected to follow. We spent nearly two months writing our massive report—on which all of us, with our different backgrounds, are agreed.

This report is the truth as we see it, as best we know it, and on this, we rest.

26 27

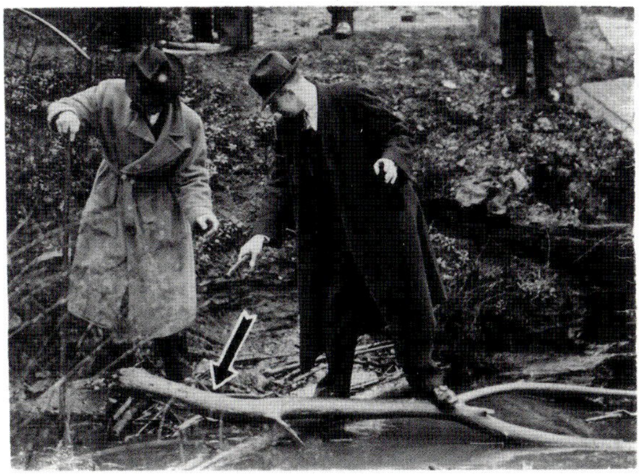

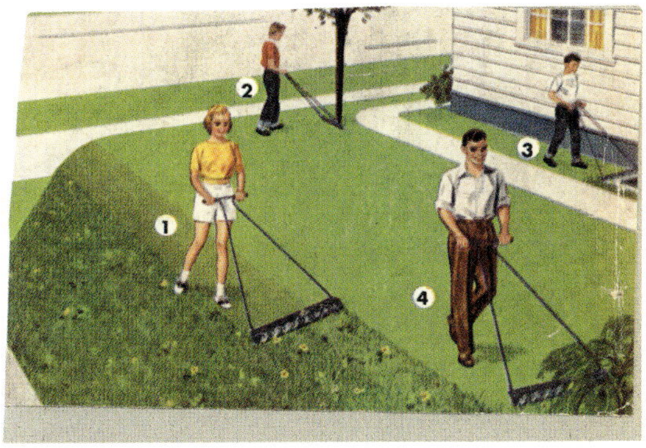

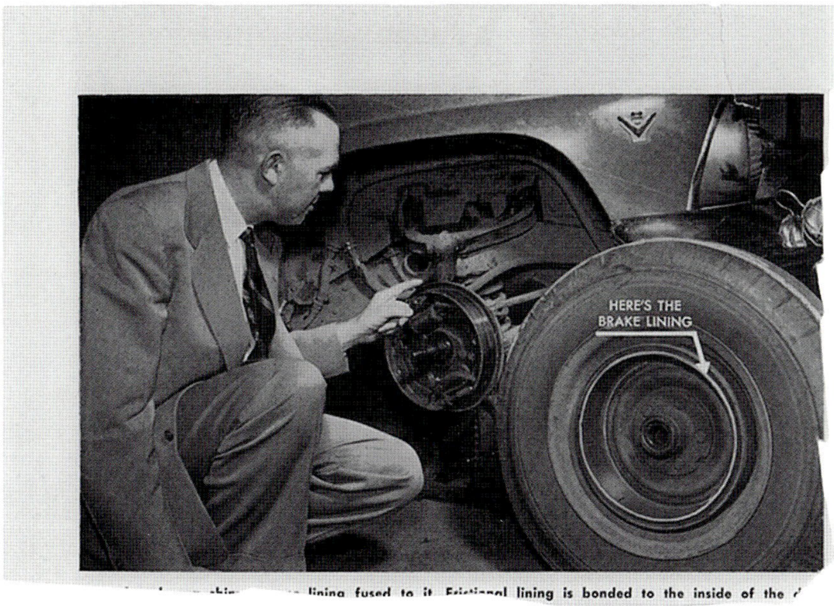

lining fused to it. Frictional lining is bonded to the inside of the

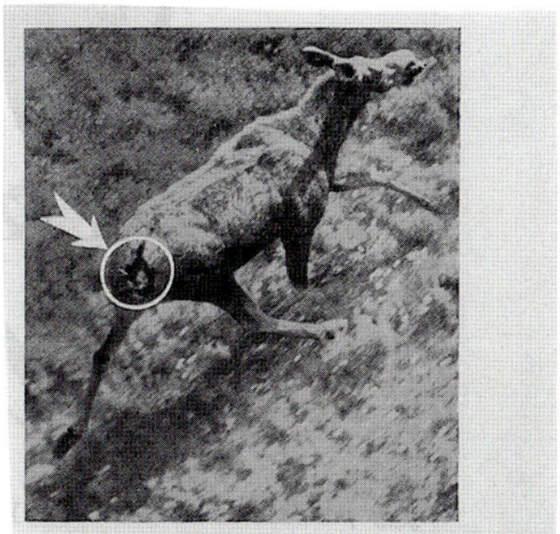
145

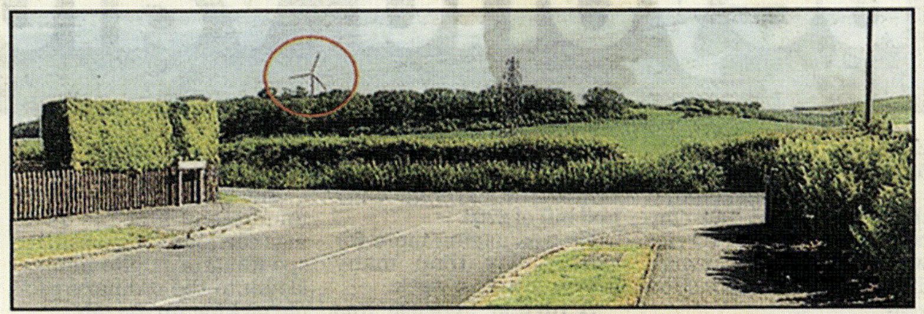
OOD

VIEW: the turb would look fro Ringme village

He said: "I have spent most of my working life making natural history films so I have seen first-hand how human beings have

fore greatly applauded the plan by Glyndebourne Opera to erect a wind turbine to help power its operations

the view wind turbines ar thought of as ugly. He sa

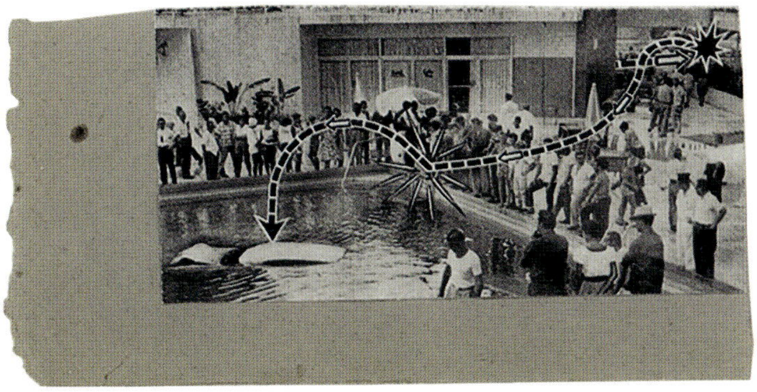

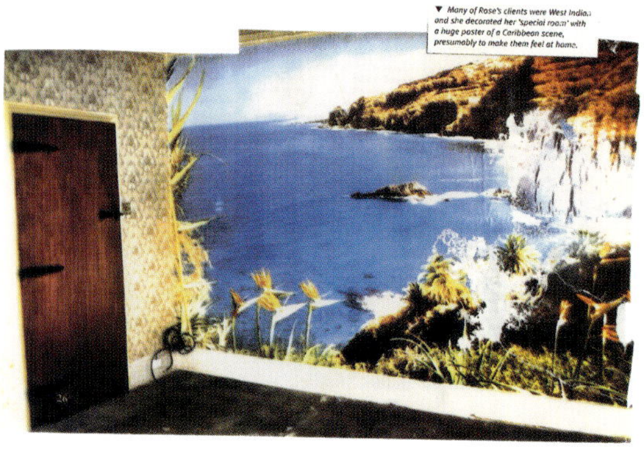

Crime – CR. 17. West interior.
Collection of Clare Strand.

of my recent work, which has enabled me to find my own system within a given proposition.

You like to find your own voice within the commission rather than feel bound by its constraints. I used *Signs of a Struggle* as a sort of bedrock for constructing a set of images about the nature of human wishes or the need to perfect. Eugene Ionesco's absurdist play *Les Tuers Sans Gages* (1957) was a useful point of departure, an expression of a utopia where the celebrants of the perfection of living deny that awful events are occurring on a daily basis. Ionesco, incidentally, mentions a photograph in the play used by the murderer to distract his victim. *Signs of a Struggle* bears reference to the crime images that I have kept on file and in my memory. This and many of my other works are partly a comment on the vanity of the quest for order. The project works well in this way, as each image and the combined text is suspended in a state of oscillation between potential readings.

What other images do you find are peculiarly charged, that remain on file, or inside your imagination? I am drawn to images that contain visual codes appearing to explain but which actually don't really help at all. An intervening arrow or a trajectory of dotted lines can make an image so much more exciting. I love Robert Groden's book *The Killing of a President* (1993), a picture anthology about the Kennedy assassination and the *Warren Report* (1964), where more detail seems to lead to greater confusion. I find the imagery of Rosa Kuleshova extraordinary as well as the portrait of Eleanor Zugan, showing the markings on flesh apparently brought about by the paranormal. I am particularly keen on imagery of illusion, magic and trickery, all of which I find innate to the photographic medium itself. I have bundles of publications, such as *Popular Mechanics* and *Healthy Living*, which contain many a photographic gem in ways of the instructional, such as the illustrative hand whose presence is crucial to the aesthetic.

In Conan Doyle's *A Study In Scarlet*, Sherlock Holmes states that there is 'no fear without imagination'. We all have this sense of the unnerving interior, the Bed and Breakfast foyer as a potential scene for violent crime, perpetuated by the artlessness of the press or crime photograph. I was fixated by the photographs of the interiors of the house of Fred and Rosemary West. I was especially interested in their keenness for photo-murals, hinting at the chasm between fantasy and reality which clearly existed.

There is always a danger of your formal exercises being regarded as pastiche, or even parody. Do you have any particular strategies to make sure you are understood, that you are not characterised as whimsical or satirical? When I make a body of work it is essential that there is oscillation between the initial proposition and its solution, otherwise there would be little point in making anything. The work is driven by my own personal response, interpretation and understanding so there will always be a shift away from what it bears reference to. Also, though there are visual similarities to the sourced material, I am making new bodies of work with a different intent and context. This in itself sets the agenda apart. I am working to my own rules.

I recognise the danger of being whimsical. I work on a fine line between my own intentions and softer readings by the audience, over which I have no control. I just have to live with that.

Can you explain here how* The Betterment Room *project fits in this sequence? I was asked to make a body of work on the theme of 'work' in modern society. *The Betterment Room–Devices for Measuring Achievement*, to give the project its full

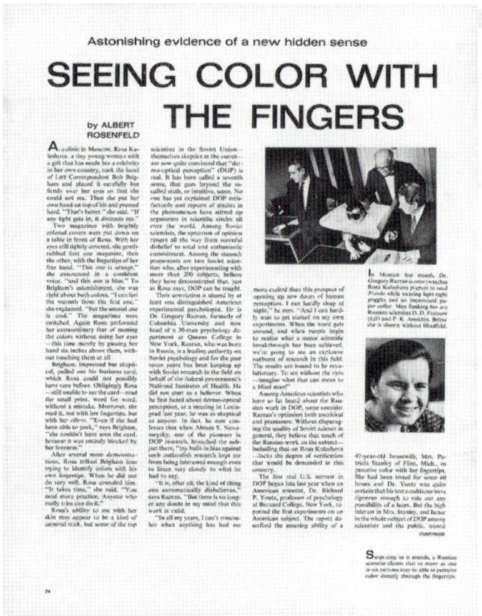
Astonishing evidence of a new hidden sense

SEEING COLOR WITH THE FINGERS

by ALBERT ROSENFELD

Paranormal – PA. 13. Rosa Kuleshova.
Collection of Clare Strand.

title, takes as a starting point Frank and Lillian Gilbreths' attempts in America, in the first part of the twentieth century, to make perfectible the constituent elements of work. The Gilbreths were the first to use photography for the measurement and enhancement of commercial endeavour, to measure units of time and motion for the 'betterment' of the worker. In their laboratory, mini-lights were attached to the workers' hands and, through the use of long shutter speeds, they would analyse the trajectories of the workers' movement.

For this project I wanted to acknowledge how our attitudes have changed towards work – how manual labour, such as grading tomatoes and sorting washers (as studied by the Gilbreths) has been displaced by other, more mysterious, activity. I became interested in the intangibility of work, seeking ways to express this through photography.

My way of synthesising all this was to apply my visual system to claims made today by *Healthy Living* catalogues, which are widely distributed as direct mail in the UK. The catalogues have fascinating instructional codes of visual language used to describe the claims made of the objects. They propose that the advertised products are a sure key to a better life, to individual fulfilment; products such as the Adult-size Meal Protector, the amazing Slimming Dress or the Deep Vein Thrombosis Cushion – all of which I purchased for my figures. In those studies for *The Betterment Room*, each person has been given an object to take into my remaking of the Gilbreths' laboratory. In contrast there is no movement, no activity, just an uneasy stasis. The apparatus of the laboratory can be glimpsed but it is fictional and on closer examination absurd and dislocated.

The *Cyclegraph* section of the project was to be a study of my own movements undertaking the mechanics of the project itself: flicking through the *Healthy Living* catalogues; my triggering of the shutter in a camera as I worked. They utilise a simple self-built lighting device, named the *Eralc* lumi-tracers, which were strapped to my hands. The *Cyclegraph* becomes a record of making the work, trying to evaluate my own performance. It is an exercise in absurdism that nevertheless has its pre-determined function, no matter how pointless.

If you are hesitant about the limitations of the gallery wall for images you want to show, are you interested in installations? In *The Betterment Room* exhibition I used a vitrine containing apparent reference material. There was clothing I had used in the images, the props, the catalogues, and the apparatus to generate light from the movements of the hands. This was presented as my own considered archive. It wasn't intended to make clearer, to elaborate and explain, but to generate a spirit of play – a middle ground between reference and installation, enhancing the pseudo-scientific surface of the work and adding to the mystery of the overall display.

I am interested in ways the project came about as a result of oblique and mysterious references rather than a conscious strategy proceeding from a logical pattern of thinking. It is often thought that, to do justice to a job, you have to research long and deeply. Yet the most profitable research could be, for example, the identification of a characteristic colour that summarises the

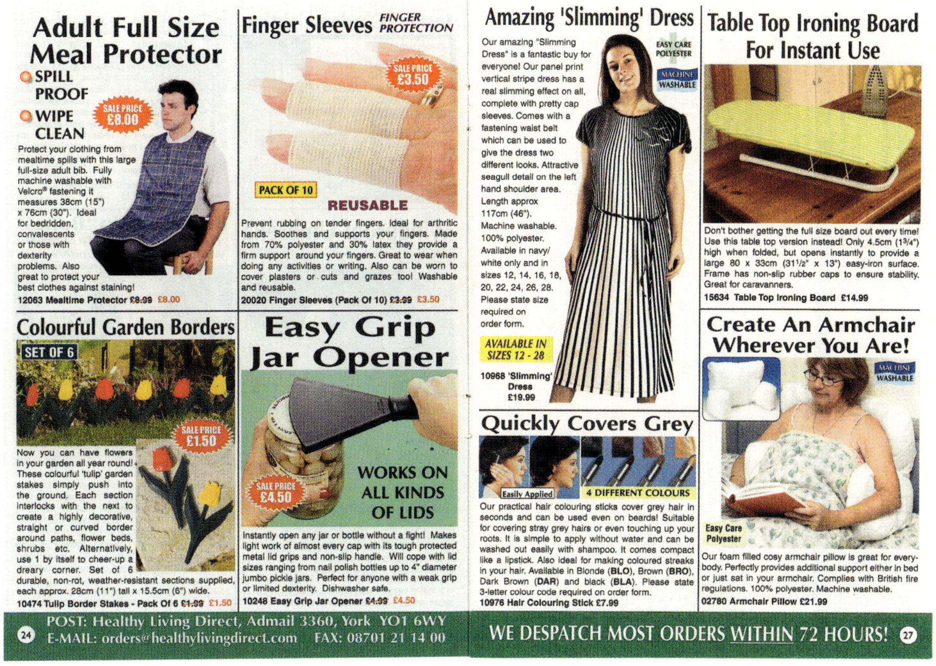

Healthy Living Catalogue Collection. 1/87. Collection of Clare Strand.

Time And Motion – TM. 3-47.
Collection of Clare Strand.

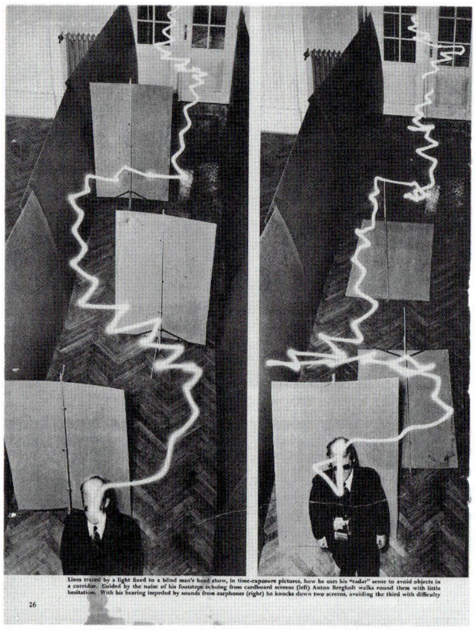

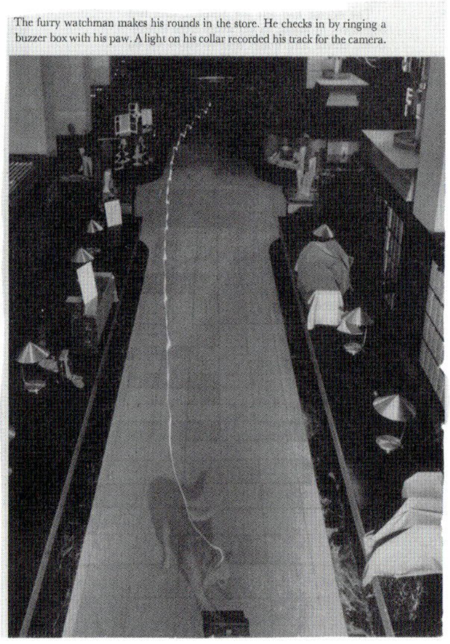

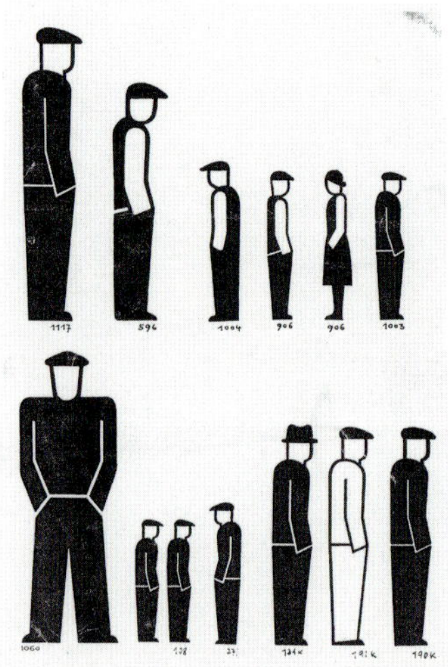

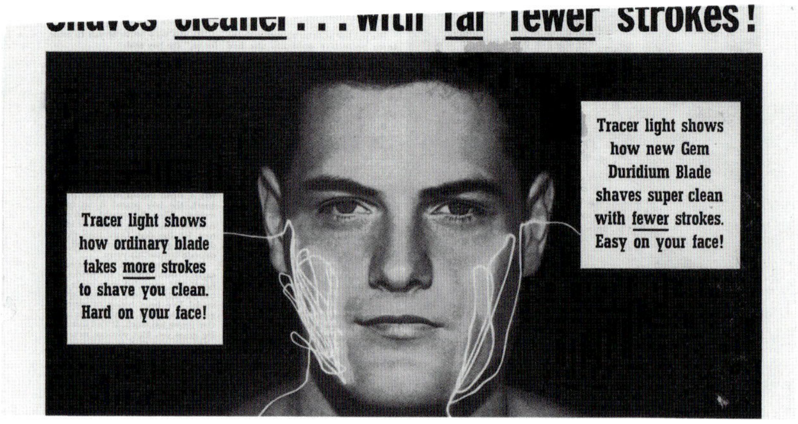

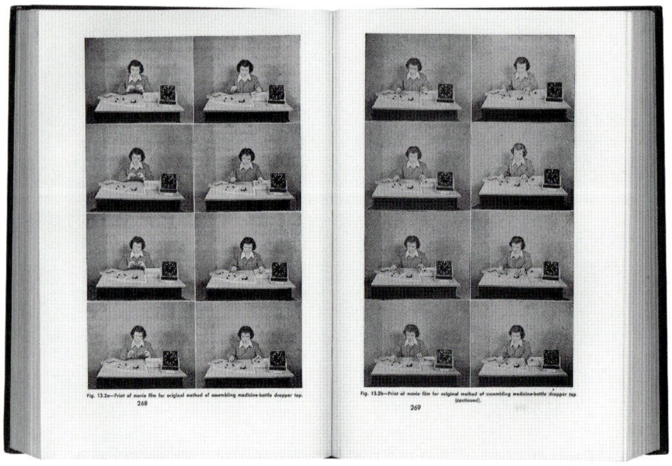

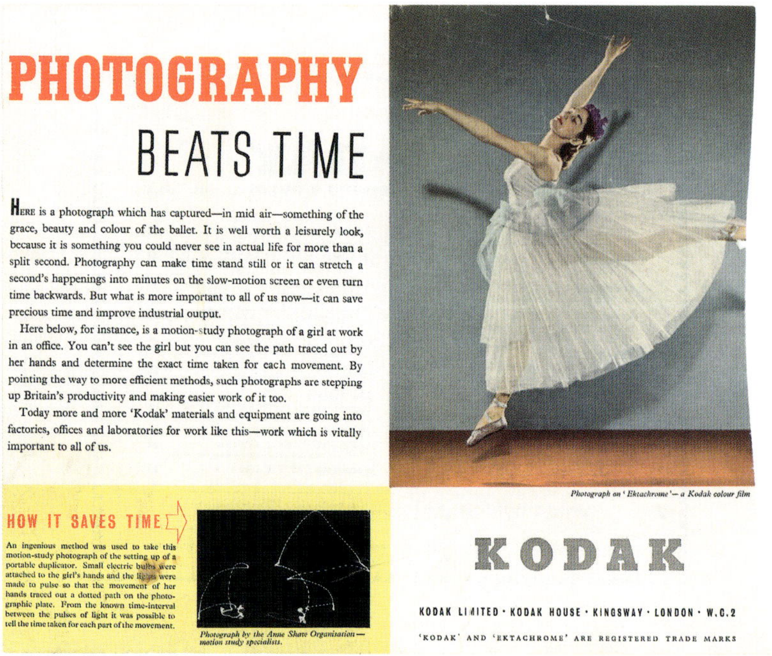

Illusions/Spirit – ILL. 17-59.
Collection of Clare Strand.

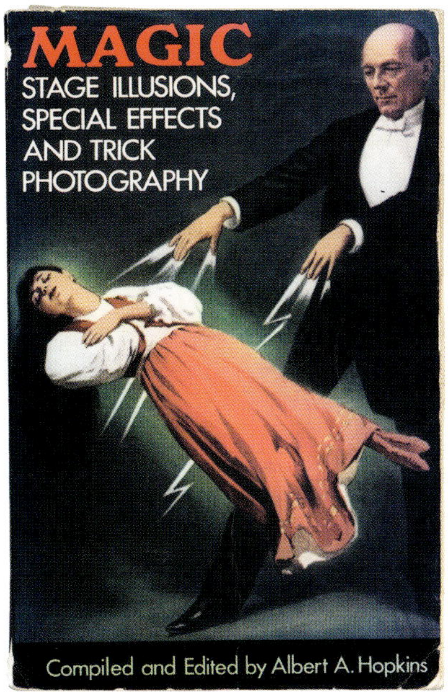

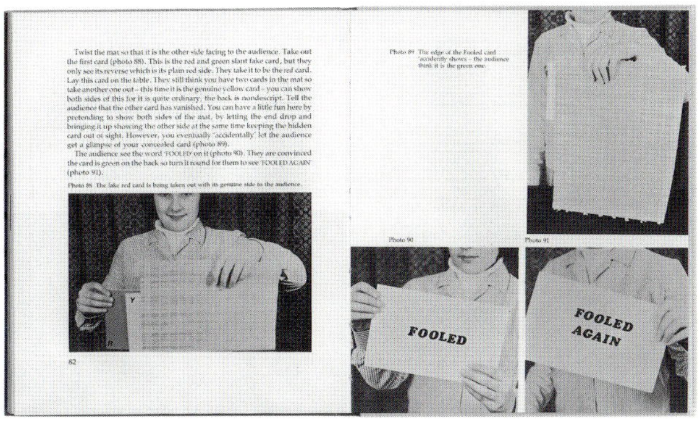

Twist the mat so that it is the other side facing to the audience. Take out the first card (photo 88). This is the red and green slant fake card, but they only see its reverse which is its plain red side. They take it to be the red card. Lay this card on the table. They still think you have two cards in the mat so take another one out – this time it is the genuine yellow card – you can show both sides of this for it is quite ordinary, the back is nondescript. Tell the audience that the other card has vanished. You can have a little fun here by pretending to show both sides of the mat, by letting the end drop and bringing it up showing the other side at the same time keeping the hidden card out of sight. However, you eventually 'accidentally' let the audience get a glimpse of your concealed card (photo 89).

The audience see the word 'FOOLED' on it (photo 90). They are convinced the card is green on the back so turn it round for them to see 'FOOLED AGAIN' (photo 91).

Photo 88 The fake red card is being taken out with its genuine side to the audience.

82

Photo 89 The edge of the Fooled card 'accidently' shows – the audience think it is the green one.

Photo 90

Photo 91

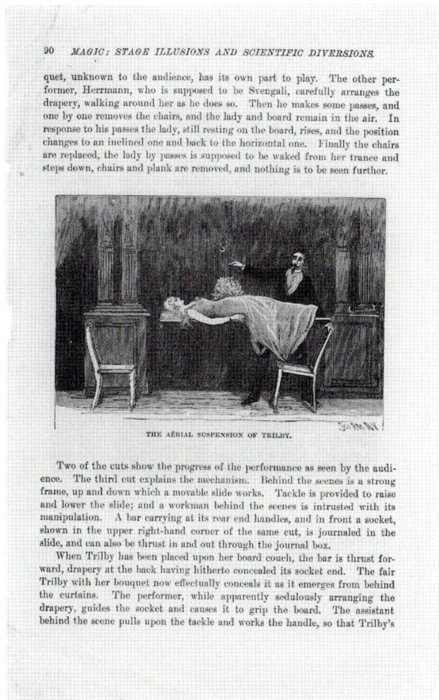

90 *MAGIC: STAGE ILLUSIONS AND SCIENTIFIC DIVERSIONS.*

quet, unknown to the audience, has its own part to play. The other performer, Herrmann, who is supposed to be Svengali, carefully arranges the drapery, walking around her as he does so. Then he makes some passes, and one by one removes the chairs, and the lady and board remain in the air. In response to his passes the lady, still resting on the board, rises, and the position changes to an inclined one and back to the horizontal one. Finally the chairs are replaced, the lady by passes is supposed to be waked from her trance and steps down, chairs and plank are removed, and nothing is to be seen further.

THE AËRIAL SUSPENSION OF TRILBY.

Two of the cuts show the progress of the performance as seen by the audience. The third cut explains the mechanism. Behind the scenes is a strong frame, up and down which a movable slide works. Tackle is provided to raise and lower the slide; and a workman behind the scenes is intrusted with its manipulation. A bar carrying at its rear end handles, and in front a socket, shown in the upper right-hand corner of the same cut, is journaled in the slide, and can also be thrust in and out through the journal box.

When Trilby has been placed upon her board couch, the bar is thrust forward, drapery at the back having hitherto concealed its socket end. The fair Trilby with her bouquet now effectually conceals it as it emerges from behind the curtains. The performer, while apparently sedulously arranging the drapery, guides the socket and causes it to grip the board. The assistant behind the scene pulls upon the tackle and works the handle, so that Trilby's

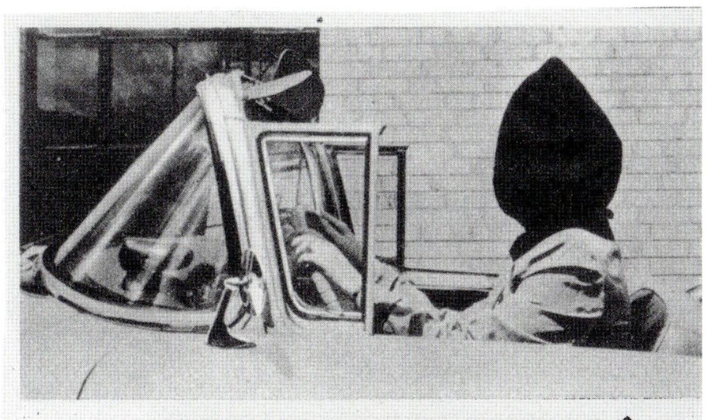

BLINDFOLDED WOMAN DRIVER, above, Mrs. Audrey Guido, astounds her neighbors in Metter, Ga., by cruising through the streets with a sack on her head. She won't tell how she manages the trick.

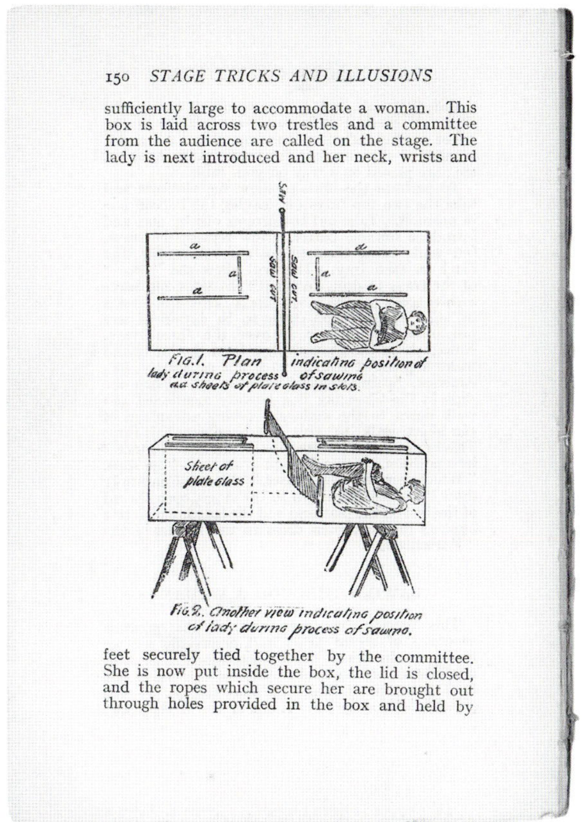

150 *STAGE TRICKS AND ILLUSIONS*

sufficiently large to accommodate a woman. This box is laid across two trestles and a committee from the audience are called on the stage. The lady is next introduced and her neck, wrists and

feet securely tied together by the committee. She is now put inside the box, the lid is closed, and the ropes which secure her are brought out through holes provided in the box and held by

The Rumanian girl, Eleonore Zugun, claimed she was the victim of a poltergeist which bit and scratched. Strange marks and swelling regularly appeared on her face and hands.

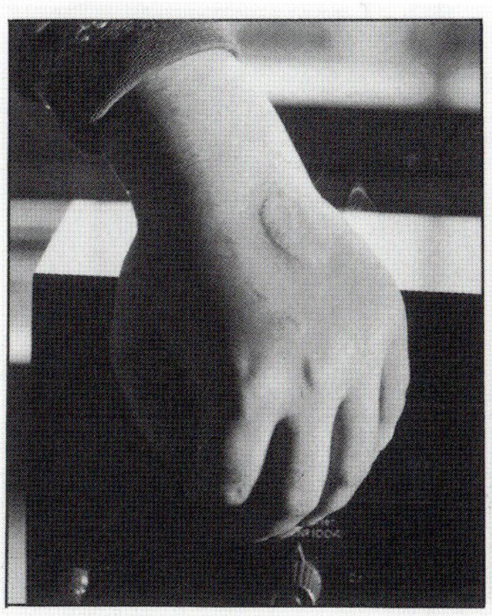

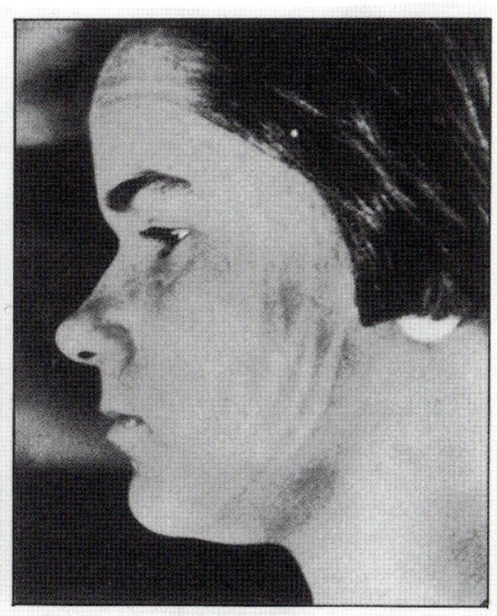

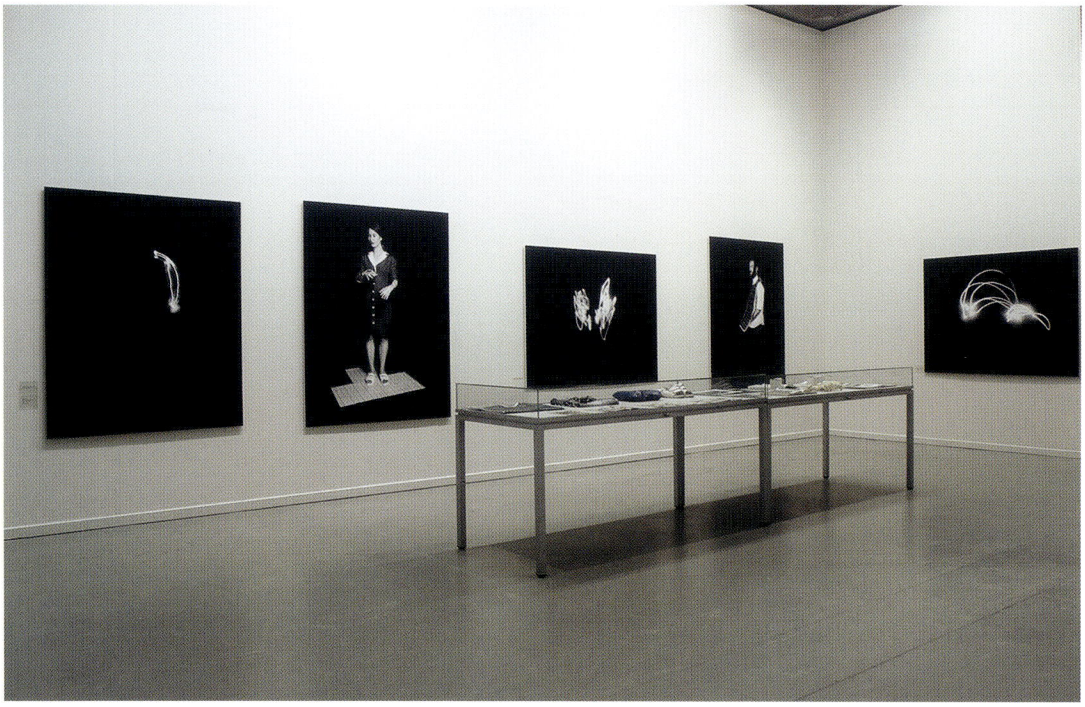

Installation image: *The Betterment Room – Devices For Measuring Achievement,* Museum Folkwang, Essen, 2005.

identity of a city, or one generation that dominates the streets, or a button-through dress or a Charlie Chaplin film still, that is key to an understanding. All the people in *The Betterment Room* project imply beige; a *Healthy Living* catalogue, though bright in appearance, is decidedly beige.

What is your attitude to the role that text plays in the contemplation of images? You have always enjoyed the possibilities that open up when text encounters imagery. You make specific references within the titles to terminology, which at first glance seems definitive (Photisms, Cyclegraphs etc).
I like the idea that a particular group of images can have a group of texts attached to it, however this doesn't necessarily mean they should provide any definitive guidance. In *Signs of a Struggle* texts were generated to accompany the images – however there is no one direct application of one to another. In tune with Ionesco's absurdist alignments, all texts apply to all images at random, creating a paradox within the general anticipated result.

So you favour 'slippage' rather than the solemn, fixed world of the caption and the imposed explanation that allows no room for ambiguity?
Slippage is a very good word to describe this – yes, slippage is something that I have tried to cultivate in my work. For instance a *Photism* is defined as a 'synesthetic visual sensation'. However once I had chosen it as my unit of terminology, the word brought about an unintended slippage into photography, away from the study of perception.

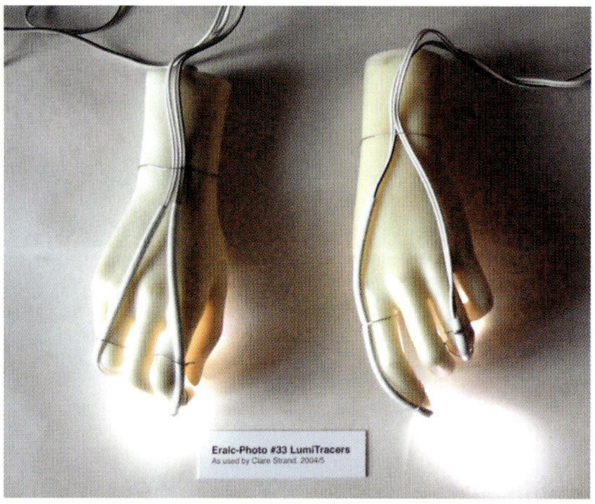

Cabinet Detail. Eralc Lumi-Tracers. Clare Strand, 2005.

In the Gilbreths' terminology there is a unit called a *Thereblig*, their name reversed as a unit of measurement, which stimulated my own version for the *Eralc* Lumi-Tracer.

***How did you then proceed into* Unseen Agents?** I felt that my early interest in the paranormal and its relationship with photography had not reached its full potential. I returned to this subject after *The Betterment Room*, as both themes share visual and historical similarities. In both areas the camera gave gravitas to the subject due to its 'scientific objectivity'. Also in both cases the camera could seemingly capture evidence of something that couldn't be otherwise seen.

Unseen Agents makes no attempt to reach a finite conclusion about the nature of the paranormal or the authenticity of its imagery. It is about the visual possibilities thrown up by this area of practice. I chose to use the Aura Camera as it embodies a belief about how photography has been understood – a mysterious magic box that can capture the essence of the sitter and bare the soul. The Kirlian process was used for the same reasons. However, in this process, there is direct physical contact with the photographic material – proposing a visual imprint of the subject or, as in my photographs, their possessions.

As I said before, the paranormal genre had obsessed me since early childhood. I read the *Fortean Times* when a teenager and later Charles Forte's book *Wild Talents* (1932), about young women, poltergeists, and the possession of telekinetic powers. I like the way Forte wrote a non-committal celebration of the strange ways of the world and I wanted this to permeate my photographs.

The Aura Polaroids were taken in a Spirit Shop at the conventional size (5x4 inches) and in colour for ten pounds each. The Aura Camera purports to bear witness to aura projection and the ethereal entity, decoded through the colours of the image. Conversely, it was only until I drained the colour away from each of the images that they started to make sense to me. A coloured aura, rendered black and white, seemed an intriguing and somewhat perverse act, much the same as showing the mechanics of the Kirlian process, without any pictorial outcome.

Now that you see your work together for the first time, what have you learnt about your own creativity and what does this imply for the future? It's difficult to assess logically where things go from here, other than to keep experimenting and to keep pushing ideas forward, perhaps in ways I can't anticipate now. My work occupies the space between the initiation of an idea and its resolution, often developing way beyond original intentions.

Major impulses for making will remain the same, getting images out of my head and making them tangible, sorting and stripping down to address the clutter in my mind, striving towards an illusive sense of clarity and order.

It's important for me to keep doing what feels right, by taking risks rather than trying to fit into any pre-defined system. This challenge will always exist hand in hand with the possibilities of abject failure.

I have invested too much in the medium to abandon it totally in favour of another, but retain the right to move to the periphery of what is generally understood as photography.

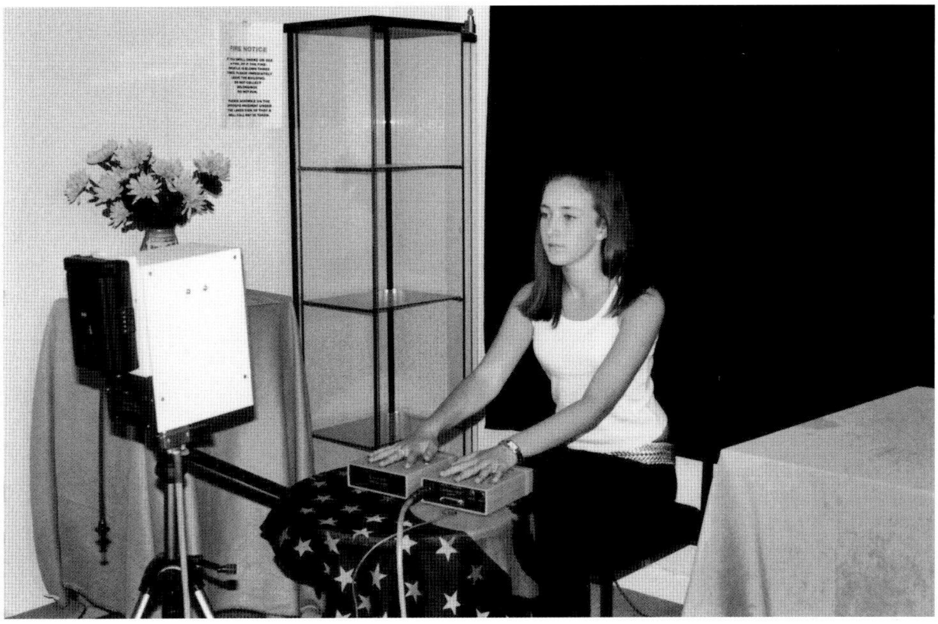

Girl having aura photographed. Clare Strand, 2007.

Conjurations
2008–2009

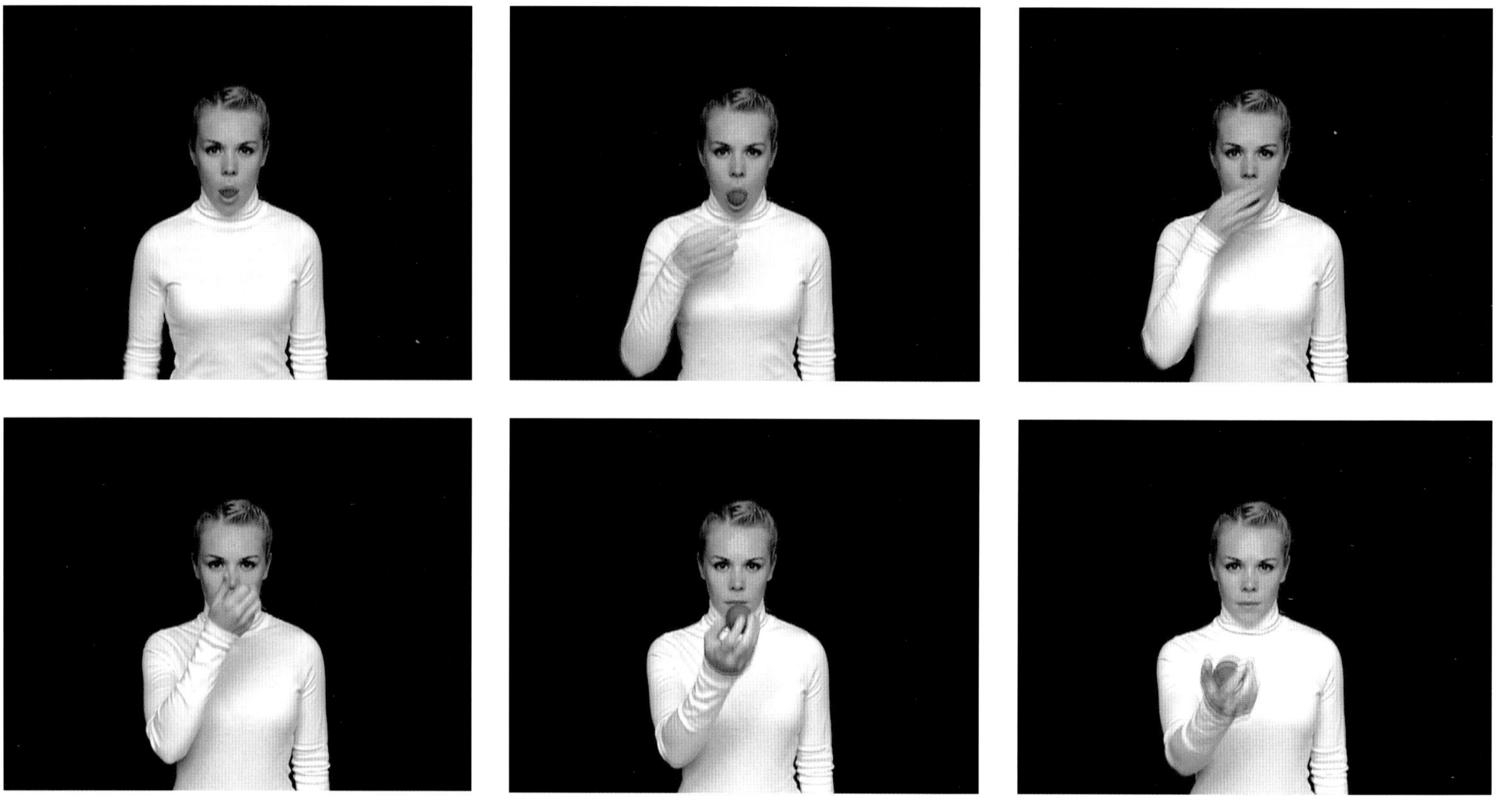

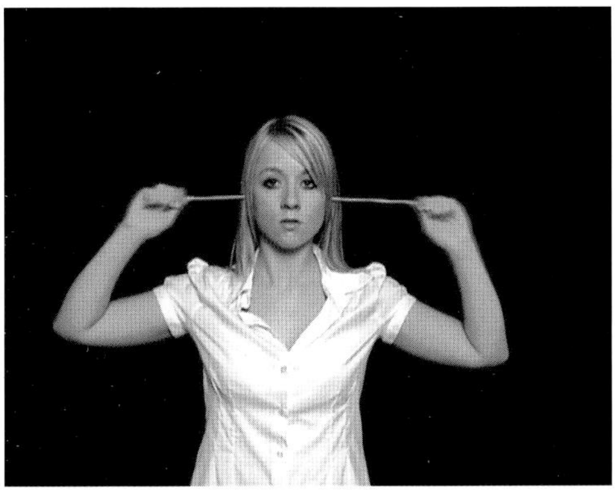
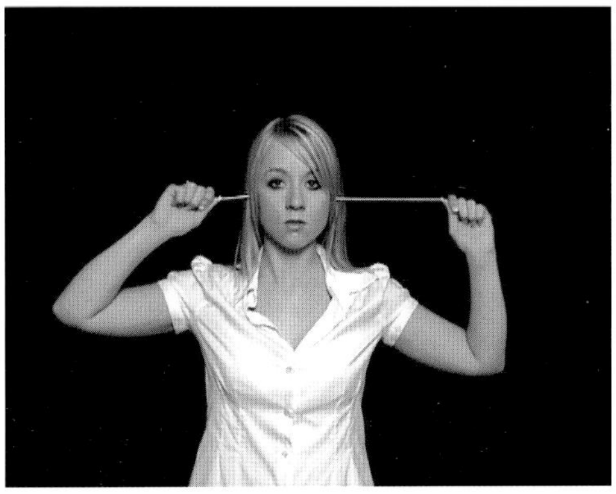
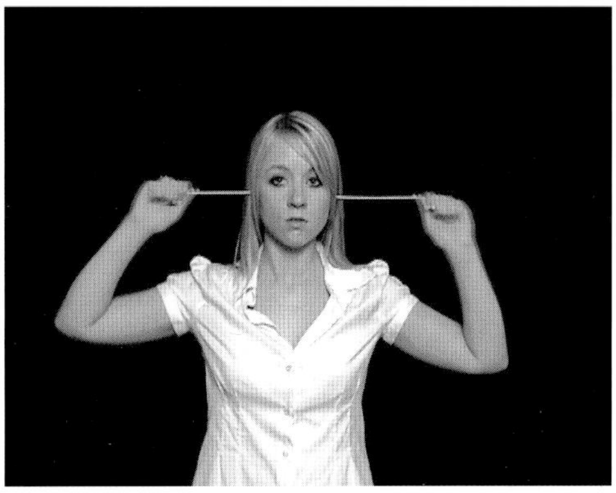
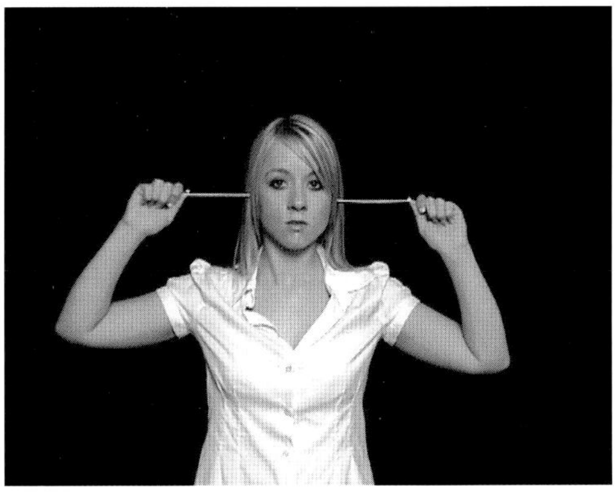
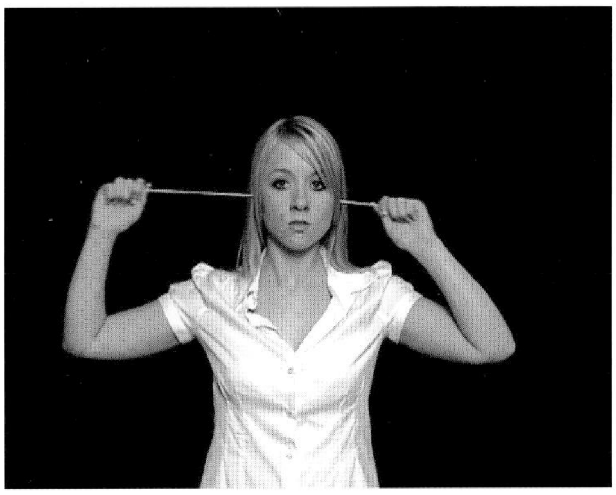
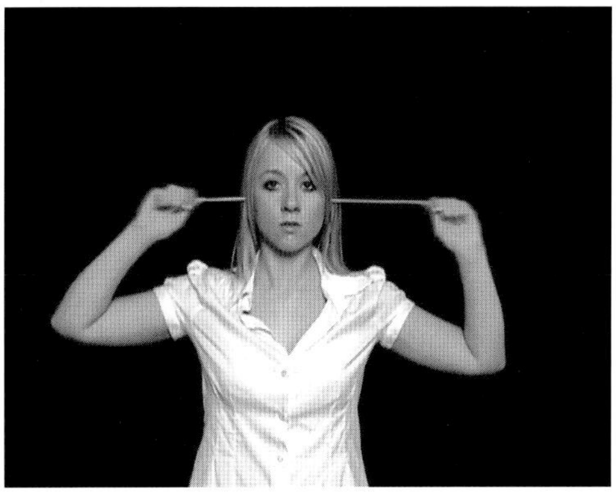

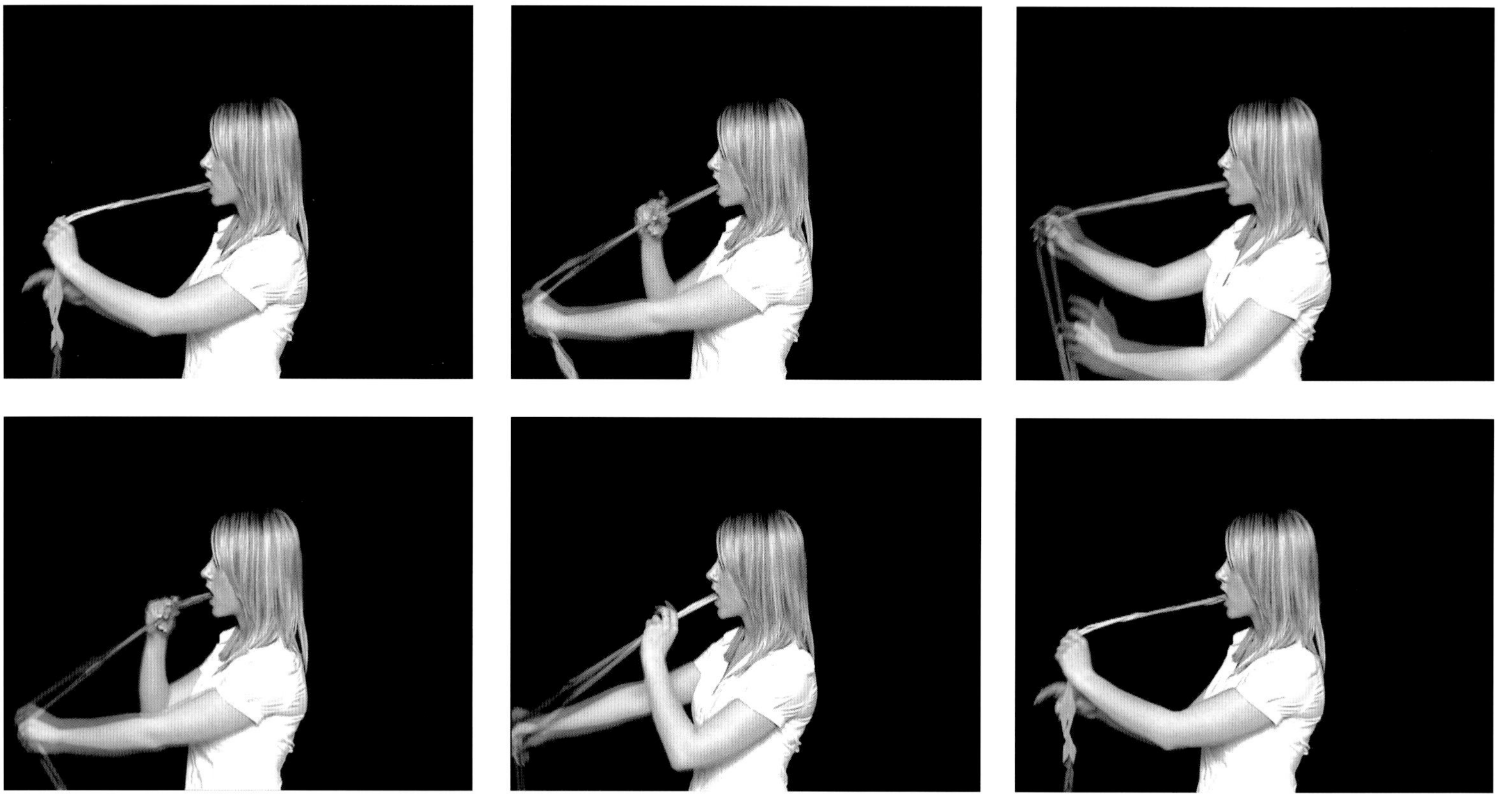

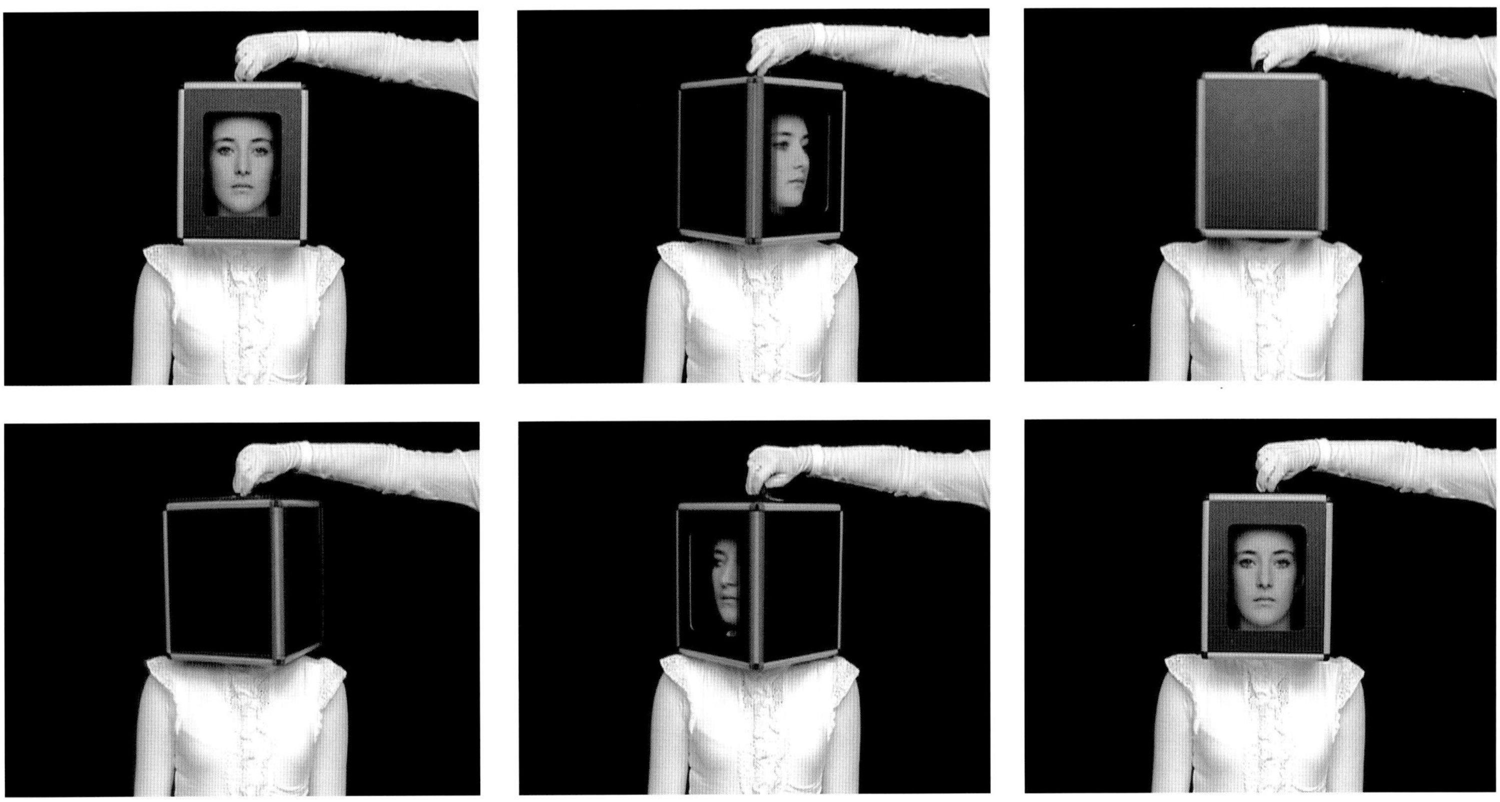

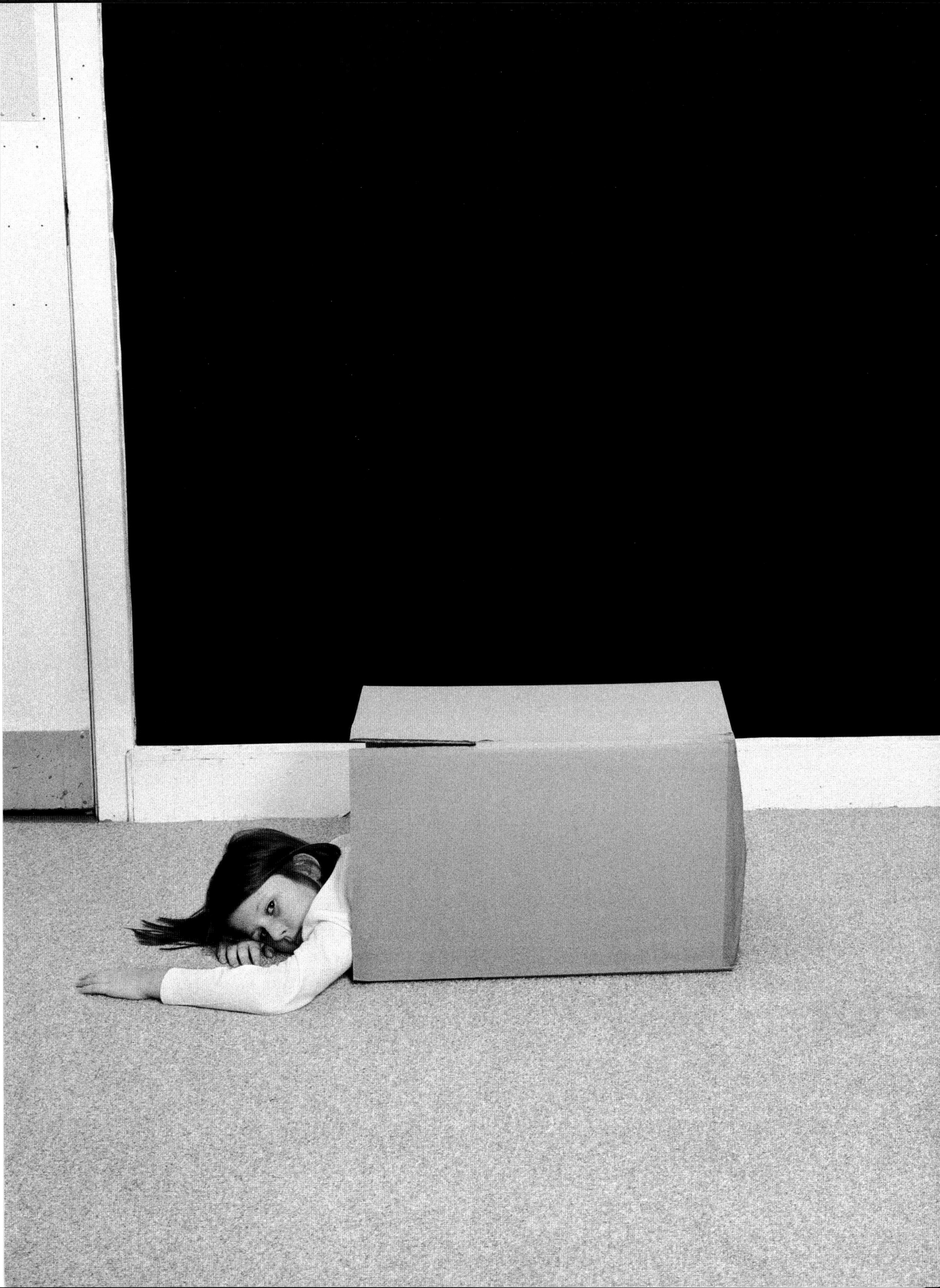

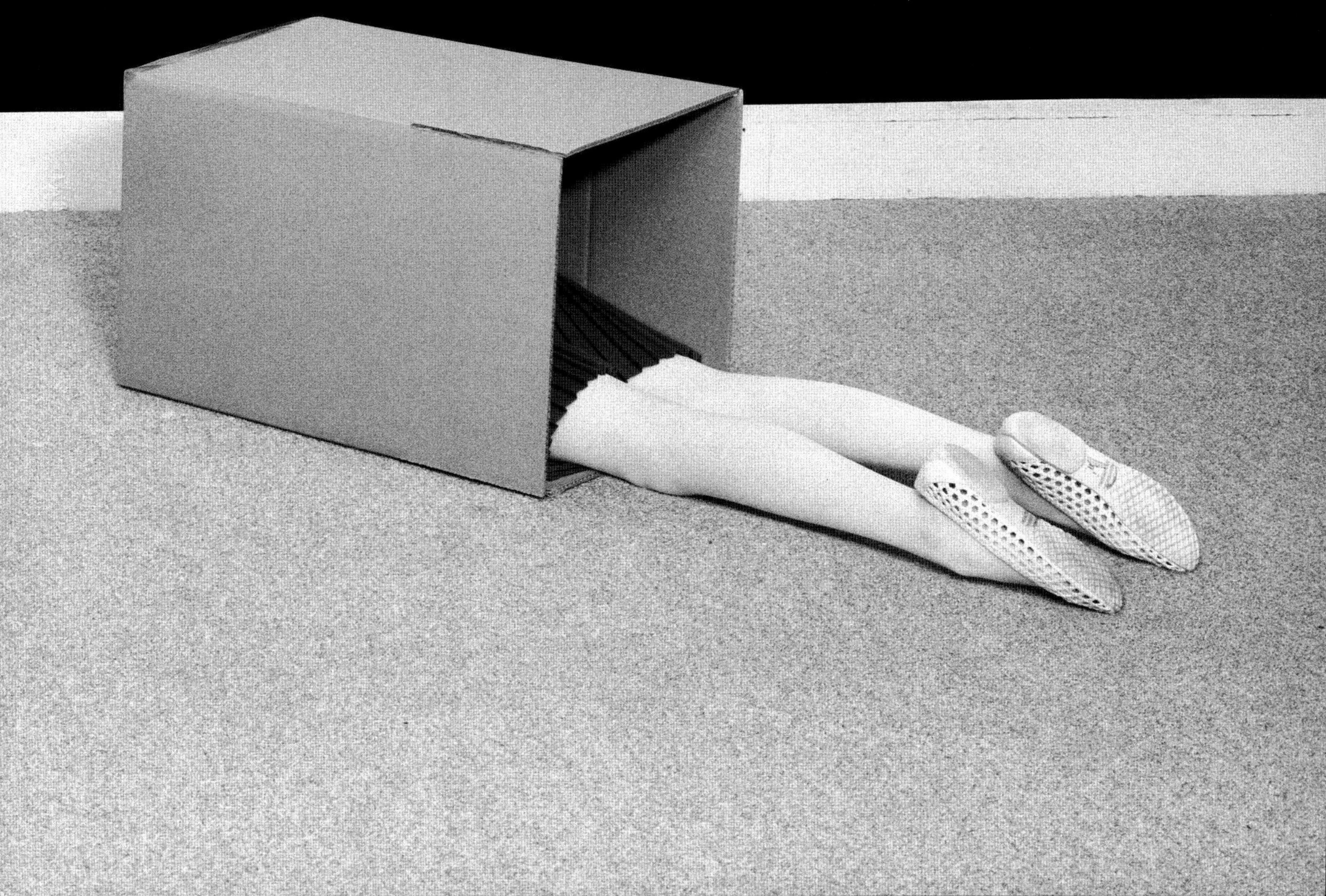

Acknowledgements

I would like to thank the following, without whom this publication would not have been possible.

Gordon MacDonald
Dolly MacDonald
Stanley MacDonald
Graham and Sandra Strand
Carolyn Strand
Dr. Chris Mullen
Val Williams
Oriole Mullen
Emma Jane Spain
Ali Warman
Mary Grigg
Lisa Hiblin

David Chandler
Rebecca Drew
Benedict Burbridge
Jane Noble
Helen Wade
and all at Photoworks

All at Museum Folkwang, especially:
Ute Eskildsen
Robert Knoldt
Christiane Kuhlmann

Ian Jeffrey
Maik Schlüter
Stuart Smith and all at Smith International.
Anna Fox
Julian Rodriguez
Anne Williams
Susie Medley

The team at Metro Imaging, London, including:
Chris Jackson
Melinda Gibson
John Waite
John Cleur
Steve Macleod

Phoenix, Brighton
Arts Council England
All at Steidl in London and Göttingen